**U.S. Department of Commerce**
National Institute of Standards and Technology

Office of Applied Economics
Building and Fire Research Laboratory
Gaithersburg, MD 20899

Users Manual for Version 4.0 of the Cost-Effectiveness Tool for Capital Asset Protection

Robert E. Chapman and Amy S. Rushing

Sponsored by:
National Institute of Standards and Technology
Building and Fire Research Laboratory

September 2008

U.S. DEPARTMENT OF COMMERCE
Carlos M. Gutierrez, Secretary

NATIONAL INSTITUTE OF STANDARDS AND TECHNOLOGY
Patrick D. Gallagher, Deputy Director

Abstract

Economic tools are needed to help the owners and managers of buildings, industrial facilities, and other critical infrastructure to select cost-effective combinations of mitigation strategies that respond to natural and man-made hazards. Economic tools include evaluation methods, standards that support and guide the application of those methods, and software for implementing the evaluation methods. This document focuses on Version 4.0 of the Cost-Effectiveness Tool (CET 4.0); it describes: the input data requirements for the software, the hierarchy of software screens, the evaluation methods employed and their associated standards, the strategy for analyzing complex decision problems, the types of reports produced, and on-line help features. Decision makers typically experience uncertainty about the correct values to use in establishing basic assumptions and in estimating future costs. When projects are evaluated without regard to uncertainty of inputs to the analysis, decision makers may have insufficient information to measure and evaluate the financial risk associated with the alternative combinations of mitigation strategies. CET 4.0 addresses uncertainty and financial risk in a structured, three-part manner. First, best-guess estimates are used to establish a baseline analysis. Second, a sensitivity analysis is performed in which selected inputs are varied about their baseline values. Third, a Monte Carlo simulation is performed to obtain an explicit measure of financial risk associated with the alternative combinations of mitigation strategies. Guidance is also given on how to choose the most cost-effective risk mitigation plan from a set of alternative combinations of mitigation strategies.

Keywords

Building economics; construction; economic analysis; homeland security; life-cycle cost analysis; risk mitigation; software

Preface

This study was conducted by the Office of Applied Economics in the Building and Fire Research Laboratory at the National Institute of Standards and Technology. The study develops a software tool for evaluating security-related investments and expenditures in constructed facilities. The intended audience is the National Institute of Standards and Technology as well as other government and private sector organizations that are concerned with evaluating how to efficiently allocate scarce financial resources among security-related investment alternatives.

Disclaimer

Certain trade names and company products are mentioned in the text in order to adequately specify the technical procedures and equipment used. In no case does such identification imply recommendation or endorsement by the National Institute of Standards and Technology, nor does it imply that the products are necessarily the best available for the purpose.

Cover Photographs Credits

Microsoft Clip Gallery Images used in compliance with Microsoft Corporation's non-commercial use policy.

Acknowledgements

The authors wish to thank all those who contributed so many excellent ideas and suggestions for this report. They include Dr. William Grosshandler, Deputy Director of the Building and Fire Research Laboratory (BFRL) at the National Institute of Standards and Technology (NIST), for his technical guidance, suggestions, and support. Special appreciation is extended to Dr. Harold E. Marshall and Mr. Douglas Thomas of BFRL's Office of Applied Economics (OAE) for their thorough reviews and many insights and to Ms. Carmen Pardo for her assistance in preparing the manuscript for review and publication. Special thanks are due to Dr. David Butry, Ms. Priya Lavappa, Ms. Jennifer Helgeson, Dr. Allison Huang, and Mr. Douglas Thomas who conducted performance testing of the software. The report has also benefited from the review and technical comments provided by Mr. Stephen A. Cauffman of BFRL's Materials and Construction Research Division and Mr. Steven Emmerich of BFRL's Building Environment Division.

Contents

Abstract iii

Preface v

Acknowledgements vii

List of Tables x

List of Figures x

1. Introduction 1
   1.1   Background 1
   1.2   Purpose and Scope 2
   1.3   Organization of this Manual 3

2. Key Concepts 5
   2.1   Overview of the Three-Step Protocol 5
   2.2   Types of Economics Decisions 6
   2.3   Economic Evaluation Methods 7
         2.3.1   Life-Cycle Cost Method 8
         2.3.2   Present Value of Net Savings 9
         2.3.3   Savings-to-Investment Ratio 9
         2.3.4   Adjusting Internal Rate of Return 9
         2.3.5   Appropriate Application of the Evaluation Methods 10
   2.4   Analysis Strategy 11
         2.4.1   Baseline Analysis 11
         2.4.2   Sensitivity Analysis 11
         2.4.3   Monte Carlo Simulation 12
   2.5   Cost-Accounting Framework 12
   2.6   Use of Case Studies 14
         2.6.1   Overview of the Data Center Case Study 14
         2.6.2   Alternatives 15
         2.6.3   Assumptions and Cost Data 16

3. Basic Features: Constructing the Baseline Analysis 19
   3.1   Getting Started 19
         3.1.1   Opening/Creating a Project File 19
         3.1.2   Cost Summary Window and Main Menu 20
   3.2   Entering Data 21
         3.2.1   Project Information 21
                 3.2.1.1   Input Cost 25
                 3.2.1.2   Event-Related Costs 28
         3.2.2   Output Window 32
         3.2.3   Alternative-Specific Features 33
   3.3   Use and Interpretation of the Data and Results Report 34
         3.3.1   Data Report 34
         3.3.2   Results Report 37
   3.4   Project Notebook 42

    3.5   Online Help 43

4.   Treatment of Uncertainty and Risk 45
    4.1   Perform Sensitivity Analysis 45
        4.1.1   Change in a Single Factor Tab 46
        4.1.2   Most Significant Factors Tab 48
        4.1.3   Change in Multiple Factors Tab 49
    4.2   Perform Monte Carlo Simulation 52
        4.2.1   Setting up the Simulation and Saving the Results 53
        4.2.2   How to Create Customized Charts and Tables 56
    4.3   Use and Interpretation of the Uncertainty Report 59

5.   Analyze Results and Recommend a Cost-Effective Risk Mitigation Plan 65
    5.1   Employ a Structured Process to Generate a Recommendation 65
    5.2   Prepare Report with Documentation Supporting Recommended Risk
        Mitigation Plan 65
        5.2.1   Suggested Format for Summarizing Results 66
        5.2.2   Creating the Executive Summary Report 69

6.   Next Step 71

Appendix A   Technical Considerations 73
    A.1   Life-Cycle Cost Method Formulas 75
    A.2   Present Value of Net Savings Formula 76
    A.3   Savings-to-Investment Ratio Formula 77
    A.4   Adjusted Internal Rate of Return Formula 78

Appendix B   Glossary Terms 79

References 105

List of Tables

Table 2-1   Summary of Appropriateness of Each Standardized Evaluation Method
        For Each Decision Type 11

Table 4-1   Summary Statistics for the Proposed Alternative Due to Changes in
        Five Factors 59

List of Figures

Figure 2-1   Overview of the Cost-Accounting Framework: Dimensions and Cost
        Types 13

Figure 3-1   Cost-Effectiveness Tool Prompt Window 19

Figure 3-2   Open Project Window 20

Figure 3-3   Cost Summary Window When Starting a New Project 21

Figure 3-4   Project Description Window for the Data Center Case Study 22

Figure 3-5   Project Alternatives Window for the Data Center Case Study 23

Figure 3-6   How to Copy the Completed Data Center Base Case into Alternative 1......24

Figure 3-7   Edit Cost/Events Window for the Data Center Case Study: Input Cost
              for the Base Case 26

Figure 3-8   Capital Investment Cost Information Window for the Data Center
              Case Study: Basic Renovation 26

Figure 3-9   O&M Cost Information Window for the Data Center Case Study: Site
              Security 27

Figure 3-10   Other Cost Information Window for the Data Center Case Study:
              Change in Traffic Pattern 27

Figure 3-11   Event Information Window for the Data Center Case Study:
              Description of the Cyber Attach Scenario for the Base Case 28

Figure 3-12   Edit Outcomes/Outcome Cost Window for the Data Center Case Study:
              Base Case Cyber Attack Outcomes 30

Figure 3-13   Outcome Information Window for the Data Center Case Study:
              Probability Information for the Base Case Cyber Attack Scenario 31

Figure 3-14   Event/Outcome Cost Information Window for the Data Center Case
              Study: Identity Theft Cost Item for the Base Case Cyber Attack
              Scenario...32

Figure 3-15   Cost Summary Window for the Data Center Case Study 33

Figure 3-16   Cover Page of the Data Report for the Case Study....................................35

Figure 3-17   Input Cost Data Summary Page of the Data Report for the Base Case 36

Figure 3-18   Event/Outcome Cost Data Summary Page of the Data Report for the
              Base Case 36

Figure 3-19   Summary of Economic Measures of Performance Page of the Results
              Report for the Case Study 37

Figure 3-20   Summary of Life-Cycle Cost Page of the Results Report for the Case
              Study 38

Figure 3-21   Summary of Life-Cycle Costs: Inputs and Event-Related Page of the
              Results Report for the Case Study 39

Figure 3-22   Summary of Costs by Alternative Page of the Results Report for the
              Base Case 39

Figure 3-23   Summary of Annual Costs by Alternative Page of Results Report for
              the Data Center Case Study 41

Figure 3-24   Summary of Annual and Cumulative Net Savings by Alternative Page
              of the Results Report for the Data Center Case Study 42

Figure 3-25   Cost-Effectiveness Tool Help Window, Help Tree, and Software Tips 44

Figure 4-1   Sensitivity Analysis Window: Using the Change in a Single Factor
              Tab to Evaluate the Impact of the Discount Rate of Life-Cycle Costs........47

Figure 4-2   Sensitivity Analysis Window: Using the Change in a Single Factor
              Tab to Evaluate the Impact of the Unit Cost of Site Security on
              Life-Cycle Costs for the Base Case 48

Figure 4-3   Sensitivity Analysis Window: Using the Most Significant Factors Tab
              to Evaluate the Impact of +/-10 % Changes of Each Factor on
              Life-Cycle Costs for the Case Study..49

Figure 4-4   Sensitivity Analysis Window: Using the Change in Multiple Factors
              Tab to Evaluate the Impact of Combinations of Factors on Life-Cycle
              Costs for the Case Study 50

Figure 4-5   Sensitivity Analysis Window: Tree Structure Showing Combinations
              of Factors Including in the Sensitivity Analysis 51

Figure 4-6   Monte Carlo Simulation Window: Using the Monte Carlo Simulation
              Window to Evaluate the Impact of Combinations of Factors on
              Life-Cycle Costs for the Case Study..54

Figure 4-7   Monte Carlo Simulation Window: Tree Structure Showing
              Combinations of Factors Including the Monte Carlo Simulation................55

Figure 4-8   Life-Cycle Costs for the Base Case and the Proposed Alternatives in
              Thousands of Dollars Due to Change in Eleven Factors 57

Figure 4-9   Present Value Net Savings in Thousands of Dollars for the Proposed
              Alternatives, Enhanced Security and Enhanced Bio Protection, Due to
              Changes in Eleven Factors 58

Figure 4-10   Saved Sensitivity Analysis Page of the Uncertainty Report for the
              +/-10 % Change in the Discount Rate 60

Figure 4-11   Most Significant Factors Page of the Uncertainty Report for the Case
              Study 61

Figure 4-12   Summary of Life-Cycle Costs and Factor Values of a Saved Change in
              Multiple Factors Page of the Uncertainty Report for the Case Study 62

Figure 4-13   Summary of Life-Cycle Costs, Probability Distributions, and Factor
              Values of a Saved Monte Carlo Simulation Page of the Uncertainty
              Report for the Case Study 63

Figure 5-1   Summary of the Data Center Case Study 67

Figure 5-2   Dialog Box for Creating the Executive Summary Report 69

1 Introduction

1.1 Background

The National Institute of Standards and Technology (NIST) is a non-regulatory federal agency within the U.S. Department of Commerce. NIST develops and promotes measurement, standards, and technology to enhance productivity, facilitate trade, and improve quality of life. In the aftermath of the attacks of September 11, 2001, NIST has taken a key role in enhancing the nation's homeland security.

NIST's Building and Fire Research Laboratory (BFRL) has as its mission to meet the measurement and standards needs of the building and fire safety communities. A key element of that mission is BFRL's commitment to homeland security. Specifically, the goal of BFRL's homeland security effort is to develop and implement the standards, technology, and practices needed for cost-effective improvements to the safety and security of buildings and building occupants, including evacuation, emergency response procedures, and threat mitigation.

The September 11, 2001 attacks on the World Trade Center and the Pentagon, and the subsequent dispersion of anthrax through the postal system, changed the way many in the United States approach security and safety. The devastation to the Gulf Coast caused by Hurricanes Katrina and Rita, and their impact on the national economy, underscored the need to plan for natural and man-made disasters as well as terrorist threats. These events have prompted the owners and managers of constructed facilities—buildings, industrial facilities, and other physical infrastructure—to address natural and man-made hazards and protect the occupants, property, and functions of their facilities.

These events have led to changes in the way key decision makers respond to natural and man-made hazards. Among these changes are the way owners and managers think about the design, location, construction, operation, and renovation of constructed facilities. The range of responses available to decision makers is extensive, as is the potential expense. Parallel to the reality of the risks posed by natural and man-made hazards is the reality of budget constraints. Owners and managers of constructed facilities are confronted with the challenge of planning for and responding to natural and man-made hazards in a financially responsible manner. The two objectives—safeguarding personnel and physical assets and satisfying financial constraints—must be balanced through a cost-effective risk mitigation plan.

Emerging from this new focus on planning is the realization that it makes sense to evaluate all kinds of natural and man-made hazards as a group. Costs for protection against multiple hazards can be shared among the hazards protected against, thereby reducing the cost of any single form of protection. Or, looked at in another way, a given cost of protection can yield extra benefits when considering multiple hazards. This spillover of benefits from one kind of protection to another highlights the need for a holistic approach to planning protection against multiple hazards.

The Cost-Effectiveness Tool (CET) incorporates and integrates research being conducted by the Office of Applied Economics (OAE) under BFRL's homeland security effort. OAE's research focuses on developing economic tools to aid facility owners and managers in the selection of cost-effective strategies that respond to natural and man-made hazards. Economic tools include evaluation methods, standards that support and guide the application of those methods, and software for implementing the evaluation methods. OAE's research has produced a three-step protocol for developing a risk mitigation plan for cost-effective protection of constructed facilities.[1] The three-step protocol has the following essential components: risk assessment, identification of potential mitigation strategies, and economic evaluation.

Risk assessment is used to identify the risks confronting a facility. It includes development of possible damage scenarios, probability assessments for these scenarios, and identification of the facility's vulnerabilities and critical areas. Identification of mitigation strategies—Engineering Alternatives, Management Practices, and Financial Mechanisms—provides performance and cost data for the possible combinations of risk mitigation strategies. Combinations of risk mitigation strategies are used to create a candidate set of alternatives for in-depth economic evaluation. The third component, economic evaluation, enables facility owners and managers to evaluate each alternative combination of risk mitigation strategies and the sequence of cash flows associated with their implementation.

1.2 Purpose and Scope

The purpose of this report is to provide documentation for Version 4.0 of the Cost-Effectiveness Tool (CET 4.0). The report serves two functions. First, as a printed copy, it is designed as a stand-alone resource for users of CET 4.0. The authors recommend users first browse through the printed copy to gain a basic understanding of the software tool. Second, this report is designed as an integral part of the software itself. Specifically, this report is integrated into the online Help feature of CET 4.0. This "Help feature" allows users to open this document while working within the software tool, enabling them to explore software-related features/capabilities, which should make the use of the software tool more transparent.

The scope of the document is limited to CET 4.0. Four earlier versions of the Cost Effectiveness Tool have been released by NIST. These earlier versions—CET 1.0, CET 1.1, CET 2.0, and CET 3.0—had different analysis and reporting capabilities. The current version—CET 4.0—represents a major upgrade in analysis and reporting capabilities. Thus, users of previous versions will experience some changes in the way they construct and analyze project files. However, the developers of CET 4.0 have designed it so that any project files saved in previous versions can be opened and saved in Version 4.0. Please note that once you save a project file in Version 4.0, it cannot be opened with an earlier version of the software.

---

[1] Chapman, Robert E., Leng, Chi J. *Cost-Effective Responses to Terrorist Risks in Constructed Facilities.* NISTIR 7073 (Gaithersburg, MD: National Institute of Standards and Technology, 2004).

Similarly, a detailed discussion of the three-step protocol is beyond the scope of this document. Readers interested in learning more about the three-step protocol, including references to risk assessment and risk management documents and software, are referred to NIST Special Publication 1082.[2]

1.3   Organization of this Manual

This report contains five chapters and two appendices in addition to the Introduction; it is designed to walk you through the features of CET 4.0 in a step-by-step fashion. Background material is first presented to insure you have a firm grounding in the concepts that underlie the software tool. Specialized analysis features are then introduced that build on and reinforce each other. Throughout this Users Manual our objective is to teach you how to use CET 4.0 to gain a deeper understanding of OAE's structured approach to the selection of cost-effective risk mitigation strategies for dealing with natural and man-made hazards.

Chapter 2 covers the key concepts underlying the CET 4.0 software tool. Topics covered include an overview of the three-step protocol and the types of economic decisions and economic evaluation methods available to decision makers. Chapter 2 shows that more than one evaluation method may be appropriate for a given type of decision. The recommended analysis strategy is then outlined. This strategy lays the groundwork for using CET 4.0 to produce a cost-effective risk mitigation plan. The cost-accounting framework is then introduced. It provides a methodology for tracking how costs affect stakeholders in different ways, and promotes a detailed, consistent breakdown of costs. The chapter concludes with a discussion of the role of case studies and a fairly detailed introduction to the data center case study, which is used throughout this report to illustrate various software features/capabilities.

Chapter 3 lays out the process by which the baseline analysis is constructed. The baseline analysis is the starting point for conducting an economic evaluation. In the baseline analysis, all data elements entering into the calculations are fixed. The term baseline analysis is used to denote a complete analysis in all respects but one; it does not address the effects of uncertainty. Constructing the baseline analysis is illustrated via a "guided tour" of the software tool's basic features. These features include entering data, editing data, and viewing preliminary results. Special emphasis is placed on how to use two key reports to verify data inputs and interpret the results of the baseline analysis. Emphasis is also placed on the Project Notebook software feature. The Project Notebook is an important resource for documenting the sources of key data elements.

Chapter 4 covers the treatment of uncertainty and risk. The concept of financial risk— the probability of investing in a project whose economic outcome is different from what is desired or expected—plays an important role throughout Chapter 4. The importance of conducting a structured sensitivity analysis is first discussed. Special emphasis is placed

---

[2] Thomas, Douglas S., and Chapman, Robert E. *A Guide to Printed and Electronic Resources for Developing a Cost-Effective Risk Mitigation Plan for New and Existing Constructed Facilities.* NIST Special Publication 1082 (Gaithersburg, MD: National Institute of Standards and Technology, 2008).

on how CET 4.0 provides a framework for analyzing both the impacts of single factors and combinations of factors on project costs. Monte Carlo simulation is then discussed with particular emphasis on how it leads to quantitative measures of financial risk. Both methods—sensitivity analysis and Monte Carlo simulation—include discussions of how to input the required data and save calculated results. The chapter concludes with a discussion of the Uncertainty Report, a key resource document for analyzing how uncertainty impacts the choice of the most cost-effective risk mitigation plan.

Chapter 5 summarizes why choosing among alternatives designed to reduce the impacts of natural and man-made hazards is more complicated than most building investment decisions. The focus of Chapter 5 is on providing guidance to help identify key characteristics (e.g., dollar-denominated impacts as well as any significant effects that remain unquantified) and the level of effort that will promote a better-informed decision. The chapter describes two methods for summarizing results for presentation to senior management and other decision makers. First, a generic format for summarizing results is presented; the generic format is based on ASTM Standard E 2204.[3] Second, the CET Executive Summary Report is described—both how to create it and how to use it to communicate results. Results from the data center case study are used to highlight key features of each method.

Chapter 6 concludes with a discussion of suggested next steps for making more effective use of the CET 4.0 software tool.

Appendix A outlines the life-cycle cost methodology and provides formulas for each of the key measures of economic performance.

Appendix B is a glossary of terms. Appendix B includes definitions of all of the key terms used throughout this Users Manual. It also includes a Notes section linking the term to software inputs and outputs as well as links to specific sections of this Users Manual. The links are designed as part of the online Help feature. Where appropriate, an Examples section is also provided. The Examples section is used to refer you to specific topics covered in the data center case study.

---

[3] ASTM International. "Standard Guide for Summarizing the Economic Impacts of Building-Related Projects," E 2204, *Annual Book of ASTM Standards: 2006*. Vol. 04.12. West Conshohocken, PA: ASTM International.

2   Key Concepts

2.1   Overview of the Three-Step Protocol

Protecting constructed facilities from extreme events—fires, floods, earthquakes, and other natural and man-made hazards—is a constant challenge for facility owners and managers. Choosing among alternative protection strategies is complicated by the fact that such strategies frequently have significant up-front investment costs, result in operations and maintenance costs that are spread over many years, and impact key stakeholders in different ways. A methodology is needed to insure that all relevant costs are captured and analyzed via well-defined metrics.

To address this need, NIST developed a three-step protocol that establishes a methodology for dealing with extreme events. The methodology is documented in ASTM Standard Guide E 2506.[4]

CET 4.0 is designed as an integral part of the economic evaluation—step three of the three-step protocol. As such, it is dependent upon the data and information produced in the first two steps of the protocol. It is important to point out that the quality of the economic evaluation is only as good as the data and assumptions going into it. Thus, a brief overview of the three-step protocol is useful in establishing the foundations for a rigorous economic evaluation of risk mitigation strategies for dealing with natural and man-made hazards.

Implementing the three-step protocol requires both guidance and data. Guidance is needed to help owners and managers to assess the risks facing their facility. Data about the frequency and consequences of natural and man-made hazards are needed when assessing the risks that a particular facility faces from these hazards. Estimates of the costs of protection are needed to insure that safeguarding personnel and physical assets and satisfying financial constraints are kept in balance. Finally, guidance on the use of economic evaluation methods is needed to insure that the correct method, or combination of methods, is used. Although there is a great deal of high-quality information available on risk assessment and risk management, natural and man-made hazards, and economic tools, there is no central source of data and tools to which the owners and managers of constructed facilities and other key decision makers can turn for help in developing a cost-effective risk mitigation plan. NIST Special Publication 1082 serves as such a central source.[5]

The first step in creating a cost-effective risk mitigation plan is a risk assessment for the facility or group of facilities to be protected. This step includes specification of the

---

[4] ASTM International. "Standard Guide for Developing a Cost-Effective Risk Mitigation Plan for New and Existing Constructed Facilities," E 2506, *Annual Book of ASTM Standards: 2006*. Vol. 04.12. West Conshohocken, PA: ASTM International.

[5] Thomas, Douglas S. and Chapman, Robert E. *A Guide to Printed and Electronic Resources for Developing a Cost-Effective Risk Mitigation Plan for New and Existing Constructed Facilities*. NIST Special Publication 1082 (Gaithersburg, MD: National Institute of Standards and Technology, 2008).

decision-maker's objectives, the facilities to be protected, the natural and man-made hazards to be considered, the composition of the risk assessment team, and documentation procedures. The risk assessment involves data collection to establish the likelihood of natural and man-made hazards as well as the on-site collection and documentation of facility vulnerabilities to those hazards. Estimates of the value of the facility's assets and the consequences of an event occurring are also produced as part of the risk assessment.

The second step of the protocol focuses on identification of risk mitigation strategies. This step uses information from the risk assessment (e.g., estimates of the value of the facility's assets and the consequences of an event occurring) to identify engineering, management and financial strategies to mitigate those consequences. The costs of implementing the alternative risk mitigation strategies and the associated reductions in consequences are also produced as part of this step in the protocol.

The third step in the protocol, economic evaluation, is the means through which competing alternatives are analyzed and a cost-effective risk mitigation plan is identified. The two previous steps, concerned with risk assessment and risk mitigation, formulate the alternative risk mitigation strategies and provide the associated cost and hazard data needed to compare the competing alternatives. The economic evaluation step includes the selection of the appropriate measures of economic performance, a rigorous analysis of the alternative risk mitigation strategies, the identification of the cost-effective risk mitigation plan, and the documentation necessary to support the recommendation of that plan. The economic evaluation step places special emphasis on the treatment of uncertainty and risk on the selection of a cost-effective risk mitigation plan.

CET 4.0 promotes a rigorous economic evaluation in three interrelated ways. First, its economic evaluation methods are based on standardized practices promulgated by ASTM International. Second, the graphical user interface facilitates the entry and editing of data required to support a rigorous economic evaluation. Finally, four specialized reports are available that enable verification of input data, an iterative approach to analyzing key cost drivers, a structured approach to the treatment of uncertainty, and an Executive Summary Report for use in presenting results to senior management and other decision makers.

2.2   Types of Economic Decisions

Investment decisions associated with alternative building designs or systems are frequently project-related, where a project could be the construction of a new building, the renovation of an existing constructed facility (e.g., a bridge), or the modernization of an existing system (e.g., a heating, ventilation, air-conditioning system (HVAC) upgrade). For a given project, the decision maker has to choose among a number of competing alternatives, all of which satisfy the same functional requirements. If the project is to upgrade a building's HVAC system and to address a number of generic security concerns, then each of the alternatives being considered will satisfy the functional requirements specified by the building's owner/manager or some other designated decision maker. At a higher level of aggregation, construction-related investment decisions often involve collections of projects.

There are four basic types of investment decisions for which an economic analysis is appropriate:

(1) Deciding whether to accept or reject a given alternative/project;

(2) Identifying the most efficient alternative/project size/level, system, or design;

(3) Identifying the optimal combination of interdependent projects (i.e., the right mix of sizes/levels, systems, and designs for a group of interdependent projects); and

(4) Deciding how to prioritize or rank independent projects when the available budget cannot fund them all.

Each type of investment decision is important. First and foremost, decision makers need to know whether or not a particular alternative/project or program should be undertaken in the first place. Second, how should a particular project/program be configured? The third type of decision builds on the second and introduces an important concept, interdependence. Consequently, for a given set of candidate projects and implied interdependencies, the problem becomes how to choose the best combination of projects. The fourth type of decision introduces a budget constraint. The aim is how to get the most impact for the given budget.

2.3   Economic Evaluation Methods

Numerous methods are available for measuring the economic performance of investments in buildings and building systems. Use ASTM Standard Guide E 1185[6] to identify types of building design and system decisions that require economic evaluation and to match the technically appropriate economic methods with the decisions.

Four economic evaluation methods addressed in ASTM Standard Guide E 1185 apply to the development of a cost-effective risk mitigation plan for dealing with natural and man-made hazards: (1) life-cycle costs (ASTM Standard Practice E 917[7]); (2) present value net savings (ASTM Standard Practice E 1074[8]); (3) savings-to-investment ratio (ASTM

---

[6] ASTM International. "Standard Guide for Selecting Economic Methods for Evaluating Investments in Buildings and Building Systems," E 1185, *Annual Book of ASTM Standards: 2006*. Vol. 04.11. West Conshohocken, PA: ASTM International.

[7] For a detailed description of the ASTM life-cycle cost standard, see ASTM International. "Standard Practice for Measuring Life-Cycle Costs of Buildings and Building Systems," E 917, *Annual Book of ASTM Standards: 2006*. Vol. 04.11. West Conshohocken, PA: ASTM International.

[8] For a detailed description of the ASTM present value of net savings standard, see ASTM International. "Standard Practice for Measuring Net Benefits and Net Savings for Investments in Buildings and Building Systems," E 1074, *Annual Book of ASTM Standards: 2006*. Vol. 04.11. West Conshohocken, PA: ASTM International.

Standard Practice E 964[9]); and (4) adjusted internal rate of return (ASTM Standard Practice E 1057[10]). Readers interested in mathematical derivations of the economic evaluation methods are referred to Appendix A.

More than one method can be technically appropriate for many design and system decisions. If more than one method is technically appropriate, use all that apply, since many decision makers need information on measures of magnitude (life-cycle costs and present value net savings) and of return (savings-to-investment ratio and adjusted internal rate of return) to assess economic performance.

2.3.1   Life-Cycle Cost Method

The life-cycle cost (LCC) method measures, in present-value or annual-value terms, the sum of all relevant costs associated with owning and operating a constructed facility over a specified period of time. The basic premise of the LCC method is that to an investor or decision maker all costs arising from that investment decision are potentially important to that decision, including future as well as present costs. Applied to constructed facilities, the LCC method encompasses all relevant costs over a designated study period, including the costs of designing, purchasing/leasing, constructing/installing, operating, maintaining, repairing, replacing, and disposing of a particular design or system. Should any pure benefits result (e.g., increased rental income due to improvements), include them in the calculation of LCC.

The LCC method is particularly suitable for determining whether the higher initial cost of a constructed facility or system specification is economically justified by lower future costs (e.g., losses due to natural or manmade hazards) when compared to an alternative with a lower initial cost but higher future costs. If a design or system specification has both a lower initial cost and lower future costs relative to an alternative, an LCC analysis is not needed to show that the former is economically preferable.

Denote the alternative with the lowest initial investment cost (i.e., first cost) as the base case. The LCC method compares alternative, mutually exclusive, designs or system specifications that satisfy a given functional requirement on the basis of their life-cycle costs to determine which is the least-cost means (i.e., minimizes life-cycle cost) of satisfying that requirement over a specified study period. With respect to the base case, an alternative is economically preferred if, and only if, it results in lower life-cycle costs.

---

[9] For a detailed description of the ASTM savings-to-investment ratio standard, see ASTM International. "Standard Practice for Measuring Benefit-to-Cost and Savings-to-Investment Ratios for Investments in Buildings and Building Systems," E 964, *Annual Book of ASTM Standards: 2006*. Vol. 04.11. West Conshohocken, PA: ASTM International.

[10] For a detailed description of the ASTM adjusted internal rate of return standard, see ASTM International. "Standard Practice for Measuring Internal Rate of Return and Adjusted Internal Rate of Return for Investments in Buildings and Building Systems," E 1057, *Annual Book of ASTM Standards: 2006*. Vol. 04.11. West Conshohocken, PA: ASTM International.

In the context of CET 4.0, the alternative (i.e., a given combination of risk mitigation strategies) that results in the lowest life-cycle cost is designated as the most cost-effective risk mitigation plan.

2.3.2 Present Value of Net Savings

The present value of net savings (PVNS) method is reliable, straightforward, and widely applicable for finding the economically efficient choice among investment alternatives. It measures the net savings from investing in a given alternative instead of investing in the foregone opportunity (e.g., some other alternative or the base case).

The PVNS for a given alternative, vis-à-vis the base case, equals their difference in life-cycle costs. Any pure benefits that result (e.g., increased rental income due to improvements) are included in the calculation of PVNS, since they are included in the LCC calculation.

With respect to the base case, if PVNS is positive for a given alternative the investment is economic; if it is zero, the investment is as good as the base case; if it is negative, the investment is uneconomical.

In the context of CET 4.0, any alternative that results in a PVNS greater than zero is designated as cost effective.

2.3.3 Savings-to-Investment Ratio

The savings-to-investment ratio (SIR) is a numerical ratio whose value indicates the economic performance of a given alternative instead of investing in the foregone opportunity. The SIR is savings divided by investment costs. The LCC method provides all of the necessary information to calculate the SIR. The SIR for a given alternative is calculated vis-à-vis the base case.

The numerator equals the difference in the present value of non-investment costs between the base case and the given alternative. The denominator equals the difference in the present value of investment costs for the given alternative and the base case. A ratio less than 1.0 indicates that the given alternative is an uneconomic investment relative to the base case; a ratio of 1.0 indicates an investment whose benefits or savings just equal its costs; and a ratio greater than 1.0 indicates an economic project.

In the context of CET 4.0, any alternative that results in an SIR greater than 1.0 is designated as cost effective.

2.3.4 Adjusted Internal Rate of Return

The adjusted internal rate of return (AIRR) is the average annual yield from a project over the study period, taking into account reinvestment of interim receipts. The reinvestment rate in the AIRR calculation is equal to the minimum acceptable rate of return (MARR), which is assumed to equal the discount rate. When the reinvestment rate is made explicit, all investment costs are easily expressible as a time equivalent initial outlay (i.e., a value at the beginning of the study period) and all non-investment cash flows as a time equivalent terminal amount. This allows a straightforward comparison of the amount of money that comes out of the investment (i.e., the terminal value) with the amount of money put into the investment (i.e., the time equivalent initial outlay).

The AIRR is defined as the interest rate applied to the terminal value, which equates (i.e., discounts) it to the time equivalent value of the initial outlay of investment costs. It is important to note that all investment costs are discounted to a time equivalent initial outlay using the discount rate.

With regard to the base case, if the AIRR is greater than the discount rate (also referred to as the hurdle rate), then investment in the given alternative is economic; if the AIRR equals the discount rate, the investment is as good as the base case; if AIRR is less than the discount rate, the investment is uneconomical.

In the context of CET 4.0, any alternative that results in an AIRR greater than the discount rate is designated as cost effective.

2.3.5 Appropriate Application of the Evaluation Methods

The four evaluation methods presented in the previous sections provide the basis for evaluating the economic performance of homeland security-related investments in constructed facilities. The equations underlying the methods presented in Appendix A are all consistent with ASTM standard practices. All of the methods are appropriate for evaluating accept *or* reject type decisions. But among the methods are several distinctions that relate to the type of investment decision that the decision maker is facing.

Table 2-1 provides a summary of when it is appropriate to use each of the evaluation methods described earlier. Note that the LCC and PVNS methods are appropriate in three of the four cases. Only in the presence of a budget constraint is the use of either LCC or PVNS inappropriate and even in that case it plays an important role in computing the aggregate measure of performance.

In summary, no single evaluation method works for every decision type. First and foremost, managers want to know if a particular project is economic. Reference to Table 2-1 shows that all of the evaluation methods address this type of decision. Second, as issues of design, sizing, and packaging combinations of projects become the focus of attention—as often occurs in conjunction with budget reviews—the LCC and PVNS methods emerge as the principle means for evaluating a project's or program's merits.[11] Finally, the tightening budget picture involves setting priorities. Consequently, decision makers need both measures of magnitude, provided by LCC and PVNS, and of return,

---

[11] If incremental values of the SIR or AIRR are computed, they can be used to make design/size and packaging decisions.

provided by either the SIR or the AIRR, to assess economic performance. Multiple measures, when used appropriately, ensure consistency in both setting priorities and selecting projects for funding.

Table 2-1 **Summary of Appropriateness of Each Standardized Evaluation Method for Each Decision Type**

Decision Type	*LCC*	*PVNS*	*SIR*	*AIRR*
Accept/Reject	Yes	Yes	Yes	Yes
Design/Size	Yes	Yes	No	No
Combination (Interdependent)	Yes	Yes	No	No
Priority/Ranking (Independent)	No	No	Yes	Yes

Source: "Standard Guide for Selecting Economic Methods for Evaluating Investments in Buildings and Building Systems." E1185. ASTM International, 2005.

2.4 Analysis Strategy

Developing a cost-effective risk mitigation plan is a complicated process, entailing three distinct levels of analysis. This "analysis strategy" systematically adds increased detail to the decision-making process. The first level is referred to as the baseline analysis. Here we are working with our best-guess estimates. The baseline analysis provides a frame of reference for the treatment of uncertainty, which is the focus of the second and third levels—sensitivity analysis and Monte Carlo simulation—which systematically vary selected sets of data elements to measure their economic impacts on project outcomes, such as the life-cycle costs of competing alternatives.

2.4.1 Baseline Analysis

The starting point for conducting an economic evaluation is to do a baseline analysis. In the baseline analysis, all data elements entering into the calculations are fixed. For some data, the input values are considered to be known with certainty. Other data are considered uncertain and their values are based on some measure of central tendency, such as the mean or the median, or input from subject matter experts. Baseline data represent a fixed state of analysis. For this reason, the analysis results are referred to as the baseline analysis. The term baseline analysis is used to denote a complete analysis in all respects but one; it does not address the effects of uncertainty.

2.4.2 Sensitivity Analysis

Sensitivity analysis measures the impact on project outcomes of changing the values of one or more key data elements about which there is uncertainty. Sensitivity analysis can be performed for any measure of economic performance (e.g., life-cycle cost or present value of net savings). Therefore, a sensitivity analysis complements the baseline analysis by evaluating the changes in output measures when selected data inputs are allowed to vary about their baseline values.

The key advantage of sensitivity analyses is that they are easily constructed and computed and the results are easy to explain and understand. Their disadvantage is that they do not produce results that can be tied to probabilistic levels of significance (e.g., the probability that the savings-to-investment ratio is less than 1.0).

2.4.3 Monte Carlo Simulation

Monte Carlo simulation varies a small set of key parameters either singly or in combination according to an experimental design. Associated with each key parameter is a probability distribution function from which values are randomly sampled. The major advantage of the Monte Carlo simulation technique is that it permits the effects of uncertainty to be rigorously analyzed through reference to a derived distribution of project outcome values. CET 4.0 includes a means for automatically running Monte Carlo Simulations and displaying the results.

2.5 Cost-Accounting Framework

The flexibility of the life-cycle cost method enables us to classify and analyze costs in a variety of ways. The result is a more focused representation of costs, referred to as the cost-accounting framework. The objective of producing this framework is to promote better decision making by identifying unambiguously who bears which costs, how costs are allocated among several widely-accepted budget categories, how costs are allocated among key building components, and how costs are allocated among the three mitigation strategies. A cost-accounting framework is needed because costs affect stakeholders in different ways. Thus, knowing who bears which costs leads to a better understanding of stakeholder perspectives and helps create mutually beneficial solutions. Finally, the cost-accounting framework promotes a detailed, consistent breakdown of life-cycle costs so that a clear picture emerges of the cost differences between competing alternatives.

Costs are classified along four dimensions within the cost-accounting framework: (1) Bearer of Costs; (2) Budget Category; (3) Building/Facility Component; and (4) Mitigation Strategy. To differentiate these costs, they are referred to as cost types and cost items. Each dimension contains a collection of cost types. The cost types are used as placeholders for summarizing and reporting aggregated cost information. Each cost type is a collection of cost items. Each cost item has a unique set of identifiers that places it within the cost-accounting framework. Examples linking cost items and cost types are given at the end of each of the four "cost dimension" paragraphs. Each dimension captures the full spectrum of costs (i.e., all costs summed across each dimension add up to the same total). A schematic representation of the cost-accounting framework is given in Figure 2-1. Within Figure 2-1, each of the four dimensions of costs is listed within a box. The cost types associated with that cost dimension are listed beneath each box.

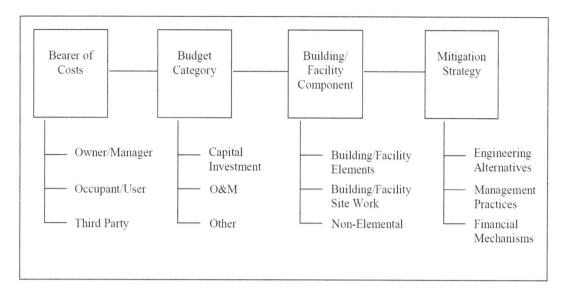

Figure 2-1   Overview of the Cost-Accounting Framework: Dimensions and Cost Types

The first dimension, Bearer of Costs, covers all stakeholder groups. A stakeholder group is defined as any collection of organizations or individuals directly affected by the project (e.g., by construction or risk mitigation activities or by disaster-related losses). The first dimension has three cost types based on who bears the costs. The three cost types are: (1) Owner/Manager; (2) Occupant/User; and (3) Third Party. Owner/Manager costs are all costs incurred by the project's owner or agent. These costs include but are not limited to design costs, capital investment costs, and selected types of repairs to the constructed facility. Occupant/User costs accrue to the direct users of the project. Occupant/User costs frequently include operations and maintenance costs and selected types of repairs not covered by the project's owner or agent. Occupant/User costs can also include delay costs and business interruption costs due to temporary closures for repair and reconstruction activities. Third-Party costs are all costs incurred by entities who are neither the project's owner or agent nor direct users of the project. One example of a Third-Party cost is the lost sales for a business establishment whose customer access has been impeded (e.g., due to a road closure during construction/reconstruction). Another example is damage to the environment from a construction process that pollutes the water, land, or atmosphere.

The second dimension, Budget Category, has three cost types based on which category of the budget the funds come from. These cost types are: (1) Capital Investment; (2) O&M (Operations and Maintenance); and (3) Other. These cost types correspond to widely used budget categories for private and public sector cost accounting. It is important to note that the dollar amounts accruing to all three cost types are inclusive of any expected losses. In the context of the previous section, Capital Investment costs accrue to the investment cost category and O&M and Other costs accrue to the non-investment cost category. All acquisition costs, including costs related to planning, design, purchase, and construction, are investment-related costs and fall under the Capital Investment cost type.

Residual values (resale, salvage, or disposal costs) and capital replacement costs are also investment-related costs. Capital replacement costs are usually incurred when replacing major systems or components and are paid from capital funds. Cost items falling under the O&M cost type include energy and water costs, maintenance and repair costs, minor replacements related to maintenance and repair, and insurance premiums paid by owners and/or occupants to reduce their risk exposure. O&M costs are usually paid from an annual operating budget, not from capital funds. Other costs are non-capital costs that cannot be attributed to the O&M cost type. An example of an Other/Third-Party cost is damage to the environment stemming from the project.

The third dimension, Building/Facility Component, has three cost types. These cost types are: (1) Building/Facility Elements; (2) Building/Facility Site work; and (3) Non-Elemental. The first two cost types are associated with the elemental classification UNIFORMAT II.[12] Elements are an integral part of any construction project; they are often referred to as component systems or assemblies. Each element performs a given function regardless of the materials used, design specified, or method of construction employed. Non-Elemental costs are all costs that cannot be attributed to specific functional elements of the project. An example of a Non-Elemental/Capital/Owner cost is the purchase of a right-of-way, or easement.

The fourth dimension, Mitigation Strategy, has three cost types. The three cost types correspond to the three risk mitigation strategies; they are: (1) Engineering Alternatives; (2) Management Practices; and (3) Financial Mechanisms. An example of an Engineering Alternatives/Elemental/Capital/Owner cost is tightening the building envelope. An example of a Management Practice/Non-Elemental/O&M/Owner cost is site security.

2.6   Use of Case Studies

The software includes a case study file, **_Data Center Case Study.lcc_**. The case study file provides a convenient frame of reference through which you can learn about the capabilities of the software and experiment with the various means of editing, creating, and deleting data elements. The case study file is designed to illustrate a wide variety of software features through a simplified, yet fairly realistic building-related example.

2.6.1   Overview of the Data Center Case Study

The case study describes a renovation project for the data center of a financial institution. The renovation is to upgrade the data center's heating, ventilation and air-conditioning (HVAC); telecommunications and data processing systems; and several security-related functions. Note that the cost estimates are for purposes of illustration only—actual renovations of different building types will face different costs and different risk profiles.

---

[12] ASTM International. "Standard Classification for Building Elements and Related Site Work—UNIFORMAT II," E 1557, *Annual Book of ASTM Standards: 2006*. Vol. 04.11. West Conshohocken, PA: ASTM International.

The data center undergoing renovation is a single-story structure located in a suburban community. The floor area of the data center is 3 716 m² (40 000 ft²). The replacement value of the data center is $20 million for the structure plus its contents. The data center corresponds to the type of structure that would be used by a major bank, credit card company, or insurance company as its primary data repository. It contains financial records that are in constant use by the firm and its customers. Thus, any interruption of service will result in both lost revenues to the firm and potential financial hardship for the firm's customers.

The site upon which the data center is located is traversed by a thoroughfare that has been used by local residents since the data center was constructed. Alternative routes are available and convenient to local residents, subject to a short detour. Plans have been made by the community to put in a new street which better links the affected neighborhoods and does not traverse the data center's site. The new street will be available for use within two years of the renovation.

2.6.2 Alternatives

The building owners wish to employ the most cost-effective risk mitigation plan (i.e., the plan that results in the lowest life-cycle cost) that will meet their objectives. Four alternative combinations of mitigation strategies are available to the building owners. All of the alternatives recognize that in the post-9/11 environment the data center faces heightened risks in two areas. These risks are associated with the vulnerability of information technology resources and the potential for damage to the facility and its contents from chemical, biological, radiological, and explosive (CBRE) hazards. Two scenarios—the potential for a cyber attack and the potential for a CBRE attack—are used to highlight these risks.

The first alternative, referred to as the Base Case, employs upgrades that meet the minimum building performance and security requirements; it is the alternative with the lowest initial investment cost (i.e., lowest first cost). The second alternative, referred to as Enhanced Security, results in enhanced security as well as selected improvements in building performance; it also provides a low level of particle filtration capability against biological agents but no gaseous capability against chemical agents. The third alternative, referred to as Enhanced Bio Protection, provides a high level of protection against particles but no gaseous protection. The fourth alternative, referred to as Enhanced Chem/Bio Protection, provides a high level of protection against particles and gaseous agents.

The three non-Base Case alternatives are referred to throughout the remainder of this report as the Proposed Alternatives. Each of the three Proposed Alternatives augments the Base Case by strengthening portions of the exterior envelope, limiting vehicle access to the data center site, improving the building's HVAC, telecommunications and data processing systems, and providing better linkage of security personnel to the telecommunications network. The main difference in the three Proposed Alternatives is their treatment of biological and chemical agents. The Enhanced Security alternative augments the Base Case by replacing existing Minimum Efficiency Reporting Value (MERV) 6 filters with MERV 11 high capacity filters and modifying the electrical feeders to accommodate higher motor horsepower. The Enhanced Bio Protection alternative augments the Enhanced Security alternative by sealing the exterior windows to make the building more airtight, replacing the MERV 11 filters with a three-stage filter consisting of a MERV 8 pre-filter, an 85 % efficient MERV 13 intermediate filter, and a 99.97 % High Efficiency Particulate Air (HEPA) filter, and modifying the electrical feeders to accommodate higher motor horsepower. The Enhanced Chem/Bio Protection alternative augments the Enhanced Security alternative by sealing the exterior windows to make the building more airtight, replacing the MERV 11 filters with a five-stage filter consisting of a MERV 8 pre-filter, an 85 % efficient MERV 13 intermediate filter, a 99.97 % HEPA filter, a 99.9 % gas phase filter, and a MERV 11 post filter, and modifying the electrical feeders to accommodate higher motor horsepower.

2.6.3   Assumptions and Cost Data

The case study covers a 25-year period beginning in 2006. Life-cycle costs are calculated using a 7 % real discount rate for the baseline analysis. Information on cost items is needed in order to calculate life-cycle costs. Cost items are classified under two broad headings: (1) input costs and (2) event-related costs.

Input costs represent all costs tied to the building or facility under analysis that are not associated with an event. Input costs include the initial capital investment outlays for facilities and site work, future costs for electricity for lighting and space heating and cooling, future renovations, and any salvage value for plant and equipment remaining at the end of the study period. Input costs are classified as either investment costs or non-investment costs.

Input costs serve to differentiate the Base Case and the Proposed Alternatives. The additional costs of the Proposed Alternatives result not only in expected reductions in event-related costs, they also reduce the annual costs for telecommunications and electricity and increase staff productivity due to improved indoor air quality. Finally, the change in the traffic pattern resulting from the enhanced renovation generates an increase in commuting costs for local residents until a new road is opened in two years.

Event-related costs are based on annual outcomes, each of which has a specified probability of occurrence. Each outcome has a non-negative number of cost items associated with it (i.e., an outcome may have no cost items associated with it if it results in zero costs). The data center case study models the risks associated with cyber attacks and CBRE attacks exclusively. The event modeling methodology, however, can also be used to model multiple hazards, such as those associated with earthquakes, high winds, or an accident resulting in widespread damage due to fire or chemical spills. Annual probabilities for the outcomes associated with each attack scenario are postulated along with associated outcome costs. The annual probabilities and outcome costs differ by renovation strategy. However, both the Base Case and the Proposed Alternatives have similar types of outcome costs. Should a cyber attack occur, it results in damage to

16

financial records and identity theft for a small set of corporate customers. Should a CBRE attack occur, it results in several non-fatal injuries, physical damage to the data center, interruption of business services at the data center, and denial of service to corporate customers during recovery.

3 Basic Features: Constructing the Baseline Analysis

This section gives you a guided tour of the basic features of Version 4.0 of the Cost-Effectiveness Tool (CET 4.0). The guided tour takes you through all of the steps required to construct the baseline analysis. Software features associated with the treatment of uncertainty and risk are covered in Chapter 4. The goal of the guided tour is for you to work systematically through the hierarchy of screens used to input, analyze, and display project-related data.

3.1 Getting Started

3.1.1 Opening/Creating a Project File

Launch the software by clicking on the CET 4.0 icon found on your desktop or by clicking CET 4.0 in the Start menu in Programs/Cost-Effectiveness Tool. The first screen to appear prompts you to create a new project file or open an existing or example project file. Figure 3-1 is a reproduction of the Prompt window. Recall that the software comes with an example file, the **Data Center Case Study.lcc** file. Thus, even when you launch the software for the first time, there is already an example project file, which you may choose to open. If you select the *Open an Existing Project* or *Open an Example Project* button, then you will be taken to the Open Project window. (Throughout this section, software features (e.g., buttons) are highlighted through the use of *italics* font.)

Figure 3-1   Cost-Effectiveness Tool Prompt Window

As a first step, open the **Data Center Case Study.lcc** file and use the *File Save As* feature to make additional copies with **lcc** extensions. Suggested file names are **test01.lcc** and **test02.lcc**. Use the test files to gain familiarity with the software. This way, if you inadvertently change or delete a data element, or create a new data element, you can go back to the **Data Center Case Study.lcc** file for the reference solution. When you use the *File Save As* feature with the case study file, the new file (e.g., test01.lcc) will be saved in the "examples" directory unless you specify otherwise. If you exit the software and later wish to open a user-created "test" file, you will need to select *Open an Example Project* from the Prompt window.

Figure 3-2 is a sample Open Project window showing the files in the "examples" directory. Note that in addition to the **Data Center Case Study.lcc** file there are two user-created "test" files: **test01.lcc** and **test02.lcc**. Highlighting the desired file and clicking the *Open* button, opens that file. Double clicking on the highlighted file opens the file as well. The Open Project window includes a *Cancel* button. If you click on the *Cancel* button, you will return to the Prompt window.

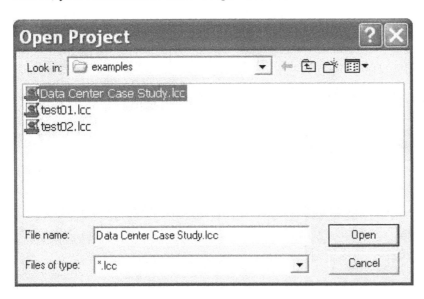

Figure 3-2   Open Project Window

3.1.2   Cost Summary Window and Main Menu

The Cost Summary window is displayed whenever a new project is created or an existing or example project file is opened. When a project is created, the Cost Summary window is blank. Figure 3-3 is an example of the Cost Summary window display when starting a new project. As you enter data into the software, the Cost Summary window displays the current value of life-cycle costs for each cost type and alternative being analyzed. It is recommended that you keep the Cost Summary window open while working in the software. If you wish to close the window, it can be reopened at any time.

The software is designed to analyze up to four alternatives (see Figure 3-3). The Cost Summary window allows you to select both the cost types and the alternatives to be included in the economic evaluation. These "choices" are represented in Figure 3-3 by the "cost type" check boxes under each dimension of the cost-accounting framework and the "alternative" check boxes in the Select Alternatives group box located in the lower left-hand corner.

A tree on the left-hand side of the Cost Summary window serves as the Main Menu to the software. The tree contains three top-level nodes: *Project, Uncertainty,* and *Reports.* Recall that software features discussed in this section are highlighted through the use of *italics* font.

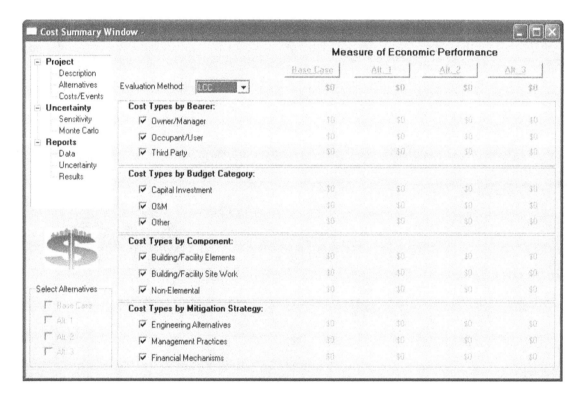

Figure 3-3   Cost Summary Window When Starting a New Project

3.2   Entering Data

3.2.1   Project Information

The options listed under the *Project* node allow you to enter project information, define alternatives, and manage cost-related information.

Clicking the *Description* option on the Main Menu opens the Project Description window. Here you can enter project information such as the project's name, a brief description of the project, the base year selected for all present value calculations, the length of the study period, whether a constant dollar or current dollar analysis is to be performed, and the discount rate. Note that when a constant dollar analysis is selected, you must use a real discount rate. This is because constant dollars have uniform purchasing power exclusive of general inflation. When a current dollar analysis is selected, you must use a nominal discount rate. Within CET 4.0, the nominal discount rate and the real discount rate are linked via a formula that includes a term for general inflation. Figure 3-4 displays the Project Description window for the data center case study. The descriptive material is designed to help decision makers differentiate among multiple projects competing for limited investment funds.

The Project Description window contains a *Notebook* icon in the bottom right-hand corner. Clicking the *Notebook* icon opens a text box, where you can enter pertinent information about the project. The material entered in the text box is designed to help you document the sources of key data elements; it becomes part of the Project Notebook Report (see Section 3.4). Notebook material suitable for inclusion under the Project Description window, includes general information associated with the risk assessment and formulation of risk mitigation strategies (i.e., steps one and two of the three-step protocol).

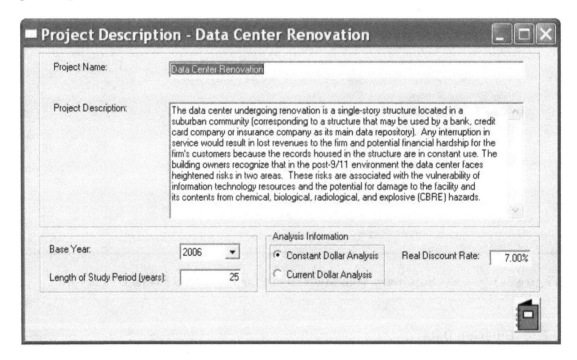

Figure 3-4   Project Description Window for the Data Center Case Study

Clicking the *Alternatives* option opens the Project Alternatives window, which allows you to add and delete project alternatives as well as enter information about the alternatives. Figure 3-5 displays the Project Alternatives window for the data center case study. The Base Case tab is selected. The window is constructed so you can switch from one alternative to another. The text box in the middle of the window allows you to enter a brief description of the alternative. The brief descriptions of each alternative serve to differentiate one alternative from another. The Project Alternatives window also contains a *Notebook* icon in the bottom right-hand corner. Notebook material suitable for inclusion under the Project Alternatives window, includes information on how the results of the risk assessment were used to formulate the risk mitigation strategies for the given alternative.

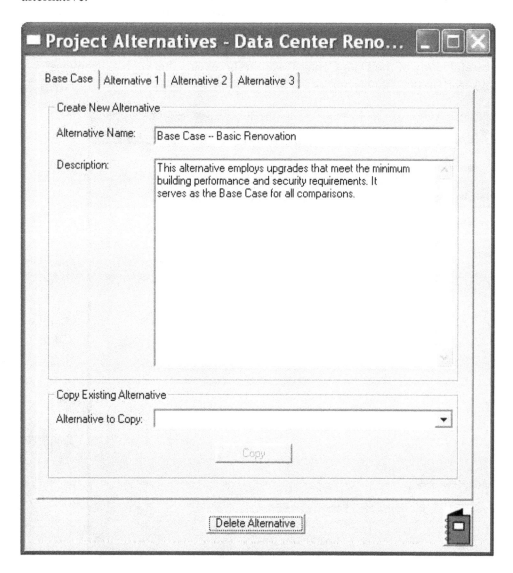

Figure 3-5   Project Alternatives Window for the Data Center Case Study

The Project Alternatives window includes a feature that allows you to copy an existing alternative to another alternative (e.g., to copy (i.e., "duplicate") the Base Case to Alternative 1). This is a powerful feature which allows you to build a rigorous Baseline Analysis of the Base Case vis-à-vis Alternatives 1, 2, and 3, using a "stepwise" approach. Use this feature with caution, however, as it is possible to "overwrite" an existing alternative. The recommended approach for using this feature is to first build a complete Base Case (i.e., a complete set of descriptive material, input costs, events, outcomes, and event/outcome costs). Once the Base Case is complete, save it, and then copy it to Alternative 1. This is done by selecting the Alternative 1 tab and then selecting the Base Case from the Alternative to Copy drop down menu in the Copy Existing Alternative group box (see Figure 3-6). Then edit the Alternative Name, Alternative Description, and any input costs, events, outcomes, and event/outcome costs for Alternative 1 to reflect its performance characteristics (i.e., ways in which it differs from the Base Case). If desired, once Alternative 1 is complete, save it, then copy it to Alternative 2 and repeat the process. A careful study of the Data Center Case Study reveals that such a "stepwise" approach can speed up the data entry process described in Section 3.2.

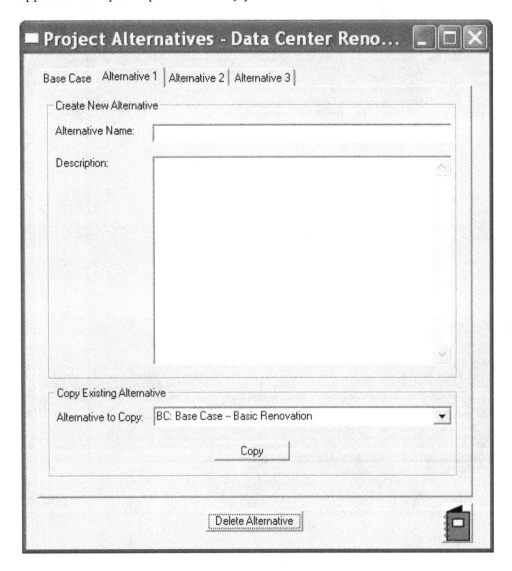

Figure 3-6   How to Copy the Completed Data Center Base Case into Alternative 1

Cost-related input screens for the software product are of two basic types: (1) input costs and (2) event-related costs. You access these screens by selecting the *Costs/Events* option on the Main Menu.

3.2.1.1 Input Costs

Clicking the *Costs/Events* option opens the Edit Costs/Events window. This screen manages the creation, deletion, and editing of input costs and event-related costs. Upon entering the Edit Costs/Events window, you must select the alternative for which information is to be reviewed or input. Both the costs and events portions of the window are active for the selected alternative. Since our focus is on input costs, however, we will address only the cost portion of the window here. The following subsection deals with event-related costs. Once the alternative is selected, the Edit Costs/Events window displays all cost items associated with that alternative. Figure 3-7 is an example of the Edit Costs/Events window for the Base Case. Notice that the input costs are listed in alphabetical order according to their Budget Category—Investment, O&M, and Other. If a large number of cost items have been entered, some costs will be hidden, but can be viewed by scrolling down the list. In this example, no costs are hidden.

Highlighting and clicking the selected cost item opens the appropriate Cost Information window. This "edit" feature allows you to review and, if desired, modify any previously recorded information for the cost item of interest. Figure 3-8 is an example of the Capital Investment Cost Information window for the data center case study. Figure 3-8 displays information on the Basic Renovation cost item, which is associated with the Base Case. Figure 3-9 is an example of the O&M Cost Information window for the Site Security cost item for the Base Case. Figure 3-10 is an example of the Other Cost Information window for the Change in Traffic Pattern cost item for the Proposed Alternative. Note that Figures 3-8, 3-9, and 3-10 include a Classification Information group box which specifies how each cost item fits into the cost-accounting framework.

The Edit Costs/Events window is the means through which new cost items are created. The creation of a new cost item is accomplished by selecting the appropriate Budget Category cost type button—*Add Investment Cost, Add O&M Cost,* or *Add Other Cost*—from the list on the right of the Costs box. The software then opens the Cost Information window associated with the selected cost type. The Cost Information windows allow you to name the cost item, generate a cost estimate via separate entries for quantity and unit cost, specify the timing of cash flows and any escalation rates that need to be applied, and add information to the Project Notebook (see Figures 3-8, 3-9, and 3-10).

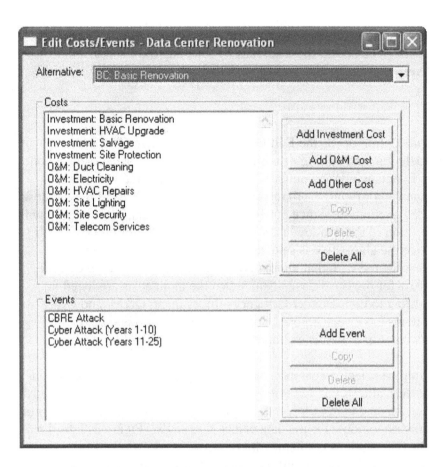

Figure 3-7   Edit Costs/Events Window for the Data Center Case Study: Input Costs for the Base Case

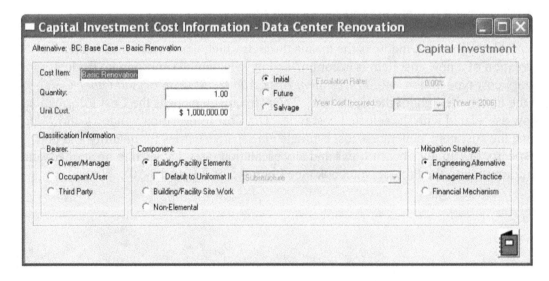

Figure 3-8   Capital Investment Cost Information Window for the Data Center Case Study: Basic Renovation

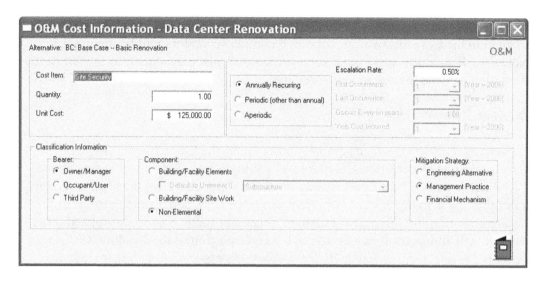

Figure 3-9 **O&M Cost Information Window for the Data Center Case Study: Site Security**

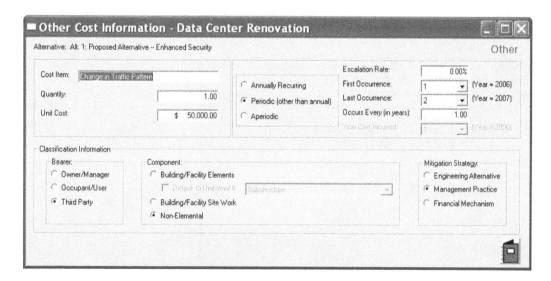

Figure 3-10 **Other Cost Information Window for the Data Center Case Study: Change in Traffic Pattern**

The Cost Information window includes an entry "field" for the Unit Cost of the cost item. In previous versions of CET, users have occasionally experienced difficulty in editing or first entering numbers in the Unit Cost field. Therefore, in order to avoid any problems editing numbers in the Unit Cost field for an existing cost item, place the cursor to the left of the first number being changed and simply type in the new number without deleting the old number. When first entering numbers in the Unit Cost field for a newly-created cost item, place the cursor to the right of the dollar ($) sign and type in your entry. You may enter a decimal point as part of your data entry, but the field will not accept a comma as part of your data entry. When you exit the Unit Cost field (e.g., by clicking on another field in the Cost Information window), comma separators will be recorded automatically. If an extra "unwanted" digit is recorded, place the cursor to the left of the unwanted digit and use the delete key to remove it.

3.2.1.2 Event-Related Costs

As noted earlier, clicking the *Costs/Events* option opens the Edit Costs/Events window. This screen manages the creation, deletion, and editing of input costs and event-related costs. Upon entering the Edit Costs/Events window, you must select the alternative for which information is to be reviewed or input. Both the costs and events portions of the window are active for the selected alternative. Since our focus is on event-related costs, however, we will address only the event-related costs portion of the window here. Once the alternative is selected, the screen displays all events associated with that alternative.

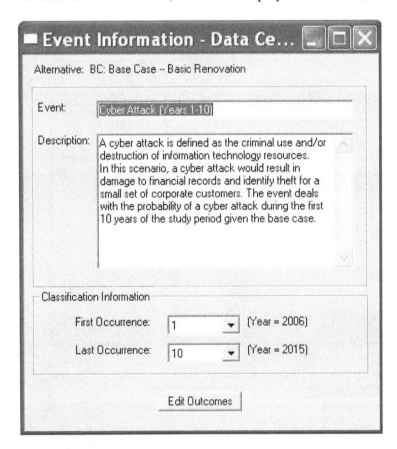

Figure 3-11   Event Information Window for the Data Center Case Study: Description of the Cyber Attack Scenario for the Base Case

Highlighting and clicking the selected event opens the Event Information window. This feature allows you to review and, if desired, modify any previously recorded information for the event of interest. The Edit Costs/Events window is the means through which new events are created. The creation of a new event is accomplished by selecting *Add Event* from the list on the right of the Events box. The software then opens the Event Information window. The Event Information window allows you to name the event, provide a brief description of the event, enter the dates of first and last occurrence, and edit event-related outcomes. Figure 3-11 is an example of the Event Information window for the Cyber Attack scenario for the Base Case. Reference to Figure 3-11 shows that this Cyber Attack scenario covers the first 10 years of the study period. A second Cyber Attack scenario covers years 11 through 25. Two time periods are used because cyber crime is on the rise and although new countermeasures are being produced regularly, hackers are becoming more adept at finding and exploiting weaknesses in countermeasures software.

Associated with each event is a set of outcomes. Information on event-related outcomes is accessed via the Edit Outcomes/Outcome Costs window. This screen is reached by clicking the *Edit Outcomes* option in the Event Information window (see Figure 3-11). Figure 3-12 is an example of the Edit Outcomes/Outcome Costs window for the first Cyber Attack scenario for the Base Case. This screen manages the creation, deletion, and editing of outcomes. The Edit Outcomes/Outcome Costs window displays all outcomes associated with the event of interest. The event/outcome costs portion of the Edit Outcomes/Outcome Costs window is initially grayed out, indicating that it is inactive. However, once an outcome is selected, the costs associated with that outcome become active. In Figure 3-12, the Attack outcome has been selected. Consequently, the outcome costs O&M: Record Reconstruction and Other: Identity Theft are active.

Highlighting and clicking the selected outcome opens the appropriate Outcome Information window. This feature allows you to review and, if desired, modify any previously recorded information for the outcome of interest. The Edit Outcomes/ Outcome Costs window is the means through which new outcomes are created. The creation of a new outcome is accomplished by selecting *Add Outcome* from the list on the right of the Event Outcomes box. The software then opens the Outcome Information window. The Outcome Information window allows you to name the outcome, provide a brief description of the outcome, assign a probability of occurrence for the outcome (outcome probabilities are a byproduct of the risk assessment), update the sum of all outcome probabilities for the event of interest, and edit outcome-related cost items. Figure 3-13 is an example of the Outcome Information window; it provides a brief description of the outcome and an outcome probability for the first Cyber Attack scenario for the Base Case.

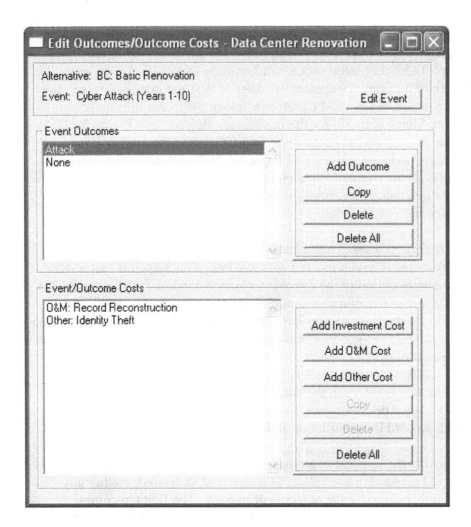

Figure 3-12   Edit Outcomes/Outcome Costs Window for the Data Center Case Study: Base Case Cyber Attack Outcomes

The Outcome Information window is also the means through which non-monetary information is input. Under certain circumstances, the effects of outcomes associated with natural and/or man-made hazards can not be expressed in monetary terms. For example, ceasing operations, staff and/or third party fatalities, and other extreme effects, are not easily valued in monetary units. The Non-Monetary group box provides the means for indicating which, if any, of these effects are associated with a given outcome. If one or more of these effects is important, check the items for which you can not estimate a dollar value. Once an item is checked, the *Enter Narrative* button is activated. Clicking the *Enter Narrative* button opens a text box, where you can enter pertinent information on that non-monetary effect. All items checked in the Non-Monetary group box, whether a narrative is entered or not, are included in the Data Report.

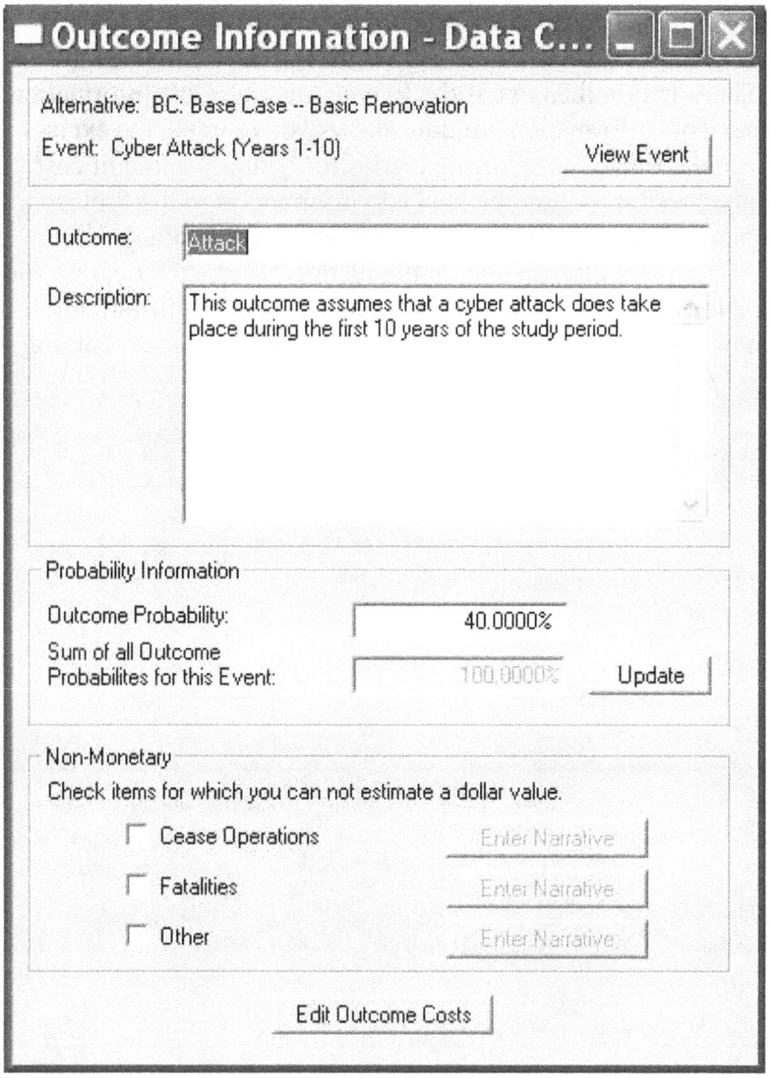

**Figure 3-13   Outcome Information Window for the Data Center Case Study:
Probability Information for the Base Case Cyber Attack Scenario**

Associated with each outcome is a set of event-related cost items. Information on event-related cost items is accessed by clicking the *Edit Outcome Costs* option of the Outcome Information window (see Figure 3-13), which opens the Edit Outcomes/Outcome Costs window. This screen manages the creation, deletion, and editing of event-related cost items. The Edit Outcomes/Outcome Costs window displays all event-related cost items associated with the outcome of interest.

Highlighting and clicking the selected event-related cost item opens the appropriate Event/Outcome Cost Information window. This feature allows you to review and, if desired, modify any previously recorded information for the event-related cost item of interest. The Edit Outcomes/Outcome Costs window is the means through which new event-related cost items are created. The creation of a new event-related cost item is

31

accomplished by selecting the appropriate Budget Category cost type button—*Add Investment Cost, Add O&M Cost,* or *Add Other Cost*—from the list on the right of the Event/Outcome Cost box. The software then opens the Event/Outcome Cost Information window. The Event/Outcome Cost Information window allows you to name the event-related cost item, generate a cost estimate via separate entries for quantity and unit cost, specify any escalation rates that need to be applied, and add information to the Project Notebook. Figure 3-14 is an example of the Event/Outcome Cost Information window for the Base Case. Figure 3-14 records information on the Identity Theft cost item for the first Cyber Attack scenario. Note that Figure 3-14 includes a Classification Information group box which specifies how each event-related cost item fits into the cost-accounting framework.

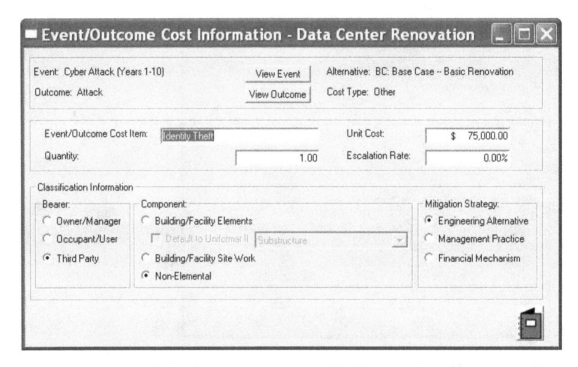

Figure 3-14   Event/Outcome Cost Information Window for the Data Center Case Study: Identity Theft Cost Item for the Base Case Cyber Attack Scenario

3.2.2   Output Window

Once all data have been input, the Cost Summary window displays the life-cycle costs for each alternative. Costs are reported for each of the four dimensions of the cost-accounting framework and for each cost type. Figure 3-15 reproduces the Cost Summary window for the completed baseline analysis for the data center case study.

The Cost Summary window provides the option for you to view calculated values for measures of economic performance other than life-cycle costs. The drop down menu in the Evaluation Method box lets you select the PVNS (present value net savings), SIR (savings-to-investment ratio), or AIRR (adjusted internal rate of return) as an alternative measure of economic performance. The PVNS, SIR, and AIRR values reported on the Cost Summary window are calculated vis-à-vis the Base Case. PVNS measures net savings of investing in the given alternative instead of investing in the Base Case. The SIR equals the difference in non-investment costs—the savings stemming from investing in the given alternative rather than the Base Case—divided by the increased capital cost for the given alternative. The AIRR measures the annual return on the additional capital investment associated with the given alternative. Thus when the PVNS, SIR, or AIRR method is selected, the only meaningful values are the ones listed under the column headings Alt. 1, Alt. 2, and Alt. 3.

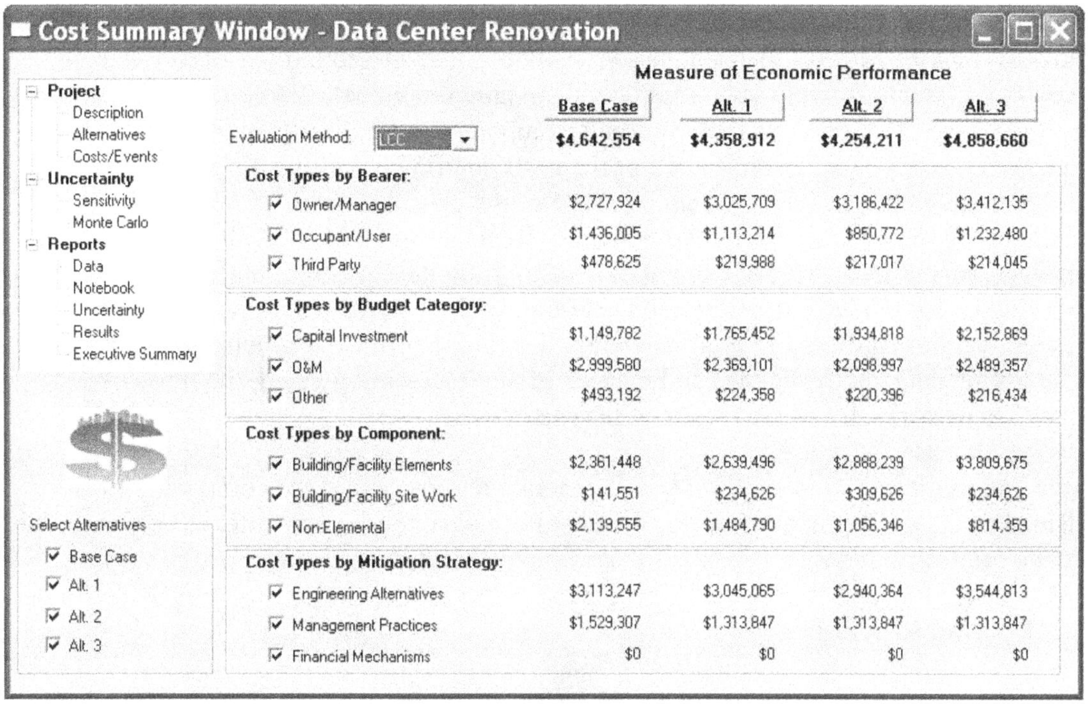

Figure 3-15   Cost Summary Window for the Data Center Case Study

3.2.3   Alternative-Specific Feature

The software also enables you to access the Edit Costs/Events window by clicking one of the alternative labeled edit buttons at the top of the Cost Summary window. In Figure 3-15 all four alternatives—Base Case, Alt. 1, Alt. 2, and Alt. 3—have data entries. Consequently, their edit buttons are active. Since each alternative has a specific edit button, when that button is active and it is clicked the Edit Costs/Events window opens with a display of all costs and all events associated with the alternative in the selected column. This feature helps you edit cost and event information very efficiently when your focus is on a single alternative.

3.3 Use and Interpretation of the Data and Results Reports

The Cost-Effectiveness Tool produces five types of reports. Although the reports share a number of similarities in terms of their content, their functions are very different. Each report is accessed via the *Reports* node on the main menu. Clicking the *Data, Notebook, Uncertainty, Results,* or *Executive Summary* option under the *Reports* node takes you to the selected report.

The Data Report is intended as a means for checking the accuracy of the information that you entered into the Cost-Effectiveness Tool. The Project Notebook Report is an important resource for documenting the sources of key data elements; it is described in Section 3.4. The Uncertainty Report contains information associated with the sensitivity analysis and the Monte Carlo simulation; it is described in Section 4.3. The Results Report is designed to help you "drill down" on how individual cost items are distributed across Bearer, Budget Category, Building Component, and Mitigation Strategy. This approach gives you a snapshot of all of the costs entering the analysis, expressed in present value terms, which "roll up" into the life-cycle costs recorded in the Cost Summary window. The Executive Summary Report is intended for submission to senior management as part of the documentation supporting the specific project being considered for funding; it is described in Section 5.2. The Results Report and the Executive Summary Report are sufficiently detailed to provide a concise snapshot of the underlying data, including the candidate set of alternatives evaluated, the types of analyses performed, and the results of those analyses.

It is important to note that CET 4.0 will generate reports only if the computer you are using has a default printer installed. It is not necessary for the computer to be connected to the printer.

3.3.1 Data Report

Clicking on the *Data* option under the *Reports* node opens the Data Report. The Data Report consists of these five sections: (1) a Cover Sheet; (2) Background Information on the project (e.g., Project Name, Project Description, Study Period, and Analysis Information); (3) Alternative Information – Descriptive Summary (e.g., Alternative Name, Alternative Description, Event Name, Event Description, Outcome Name, Outcome Description, and Key Parameters, Non-Monetary Items); (4) Alternative Information – Input Cost Data Summary (e.g., Cost Item, First Year, Last Year, Occurs Every, Bearer, Category, Component, Strategy, Escalation Rate, and Dollar Amount); and (5) Alternative Information – Event/Outcome Cost Data Summary (e.g., Event, Outcome, Event/Outcome Cost Item, First Year, Last Year, Bearer, Escalation Rate, Dollar Amount).

Verifying the accuracy of input data is essential to insure that the results of the economic evaluation are consistent with the underlying data. The Data Report is specifically designed to verify the accuracy of the input data. Figure 3-16 reproduces the Cover Page of the Data Report for the case study. The cover page includes the report title—Data Report, the project name – Data Center Renovation, and the date printed.

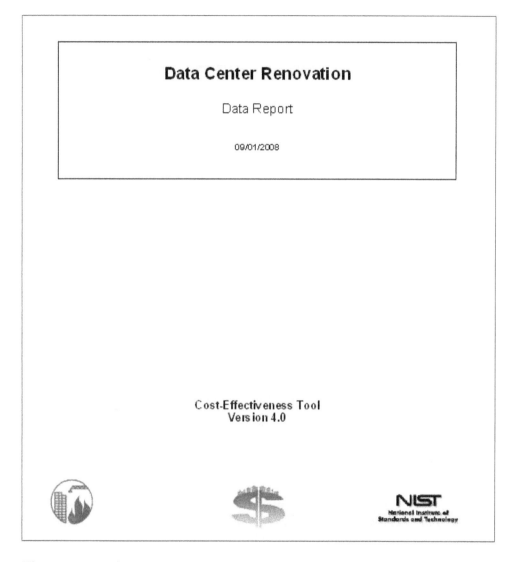

Figure 3-16   Cover Page of the Data Report for the Case Study

Figures 3-17 and 3-18 provide information on the input costs and event-related costs for the Base Case. In both figures the columns record the name of the cost item, the first and last years that cost occurs, classification information (i.e., each dimension and cost type of the cost-accounting framework), the escalation rate, and the dollar amount. Note that the dollar amount is equal to the product of the unit cost and the quantity (i.e., the number of units). Figure 3-17, which presents input cost information, includes an additional column that shows for O&M and Other costs the replacement cycle. Figure 3-18 includes additional information describing the event and the outcome to which the cost items are attached

Alternative Information - Input Cost Data Summary

Input Costs Summary: Basic Renovation

Cost Item	First Year	Last Year	Occurs Every	Bearer	Category	Component	Strategy	Escalation Rate	Amount ($)
Basic Renovation	2006	2006	1.00	Owner/Manager	Capital Investment	Building/Facility Elements	Engineering	0.00%	1,000,000.00
Duct Cleaning	2022	2022	1.00	Occupant/User	O&M	Building/Facility Elements	Engineering	0.00%	5,000.00
Electricity	2006	2030	1.00	Occupant/User	O&M	Building/Facility Elements	Engineering	-0.10%	72,000.00
HVAC Repairs	2009	2029	4.00	Occupant/User	O&M	Building/Facility Elements	Engineering	0.00%	5,000.00
HVAC Upgrade	2022	2022	1.00	Owner/Manager	Capital Investment	Building/Facility Elements	Engineering	0.00%	25,000.00
Salvage	2030	2030	1.00	Owner/Manager	Capital Investment	Building/Facility Elements	Engineering	0.00%	-10,000.00
Site Lighting	2006	2030	1.00	Owner/Manager	O&M	Building/Facility Site Work	Engineering	-0.10%	3,600.00
Site Protection	2006	2006	1.00	Owner/Manager	Capital Investment	Building/Facility Site Work	Engineering	0.00%	100,000.00
Site Security	2006	2030	1.00	Owner/Manager	O&M	Non-Elemental	Management	0.50%	125,000.00
Telecom Services	2006	2030	1.00	Occupant/User	O&M	Building/Facility Elements	Engineering	0.00%	40,000.00

Figure 3-17   Input Cost Data Summary Page of the Data Report for the Base Case

Alternative Information - Event/Outcome Cost Data Summary

Event/Outcome Costs Summary: Basic Renovation

Event: CBRE Attack

Outcome: None

No costs are associated with this outcome

Outcome: Minor

Event/Outcome Cost Item	First Year	Last Year	Bearer	Category	Component	Strategy	Escalation Rate	Amount ($)
Business Interruption	2006	2030	Occupant/User	O&M	Non-Elemental	Engineering	0.00%	250,000.00
Damage to Data Center	2006	2030	Owner/Manager	Capital Investment	Building/Facility Elements	Engineering	1.00%	80,000.00
Denial of Service	2006	2030	Third Party	Other	Non-Elemental	Engineering	0.00%	100,000.00
Non-fatal Injuries - Occupant/User	2006	2030	Occupant/User	Other	Non-Elemental	Engineering	0.00%	25,000.00
Non-fatal Injuries - Owner/Manager	2006	2030	Owner/Manager	Other	Non-Elemental	Engineering	0.00%	25,000.00
Non-fatal Injuries - Third Party	2006	2030	Third Party	Other	Non-Elemental	Engineering	0.00%	25,000.00

Outcome: Major

Event/Outcome Cost Item	First Year	Last Year	Bearer	Category	Component	Strategy	Escalation Rate	Amount ($)
Business Interruption	2006	2030	Occupant/User	O&M	Non-Elemental	Engineering	0.00%	5,000,000.00
Damage to Data Center	2006	2030	Owner/Manager	Capital Investment	Building/Facility Elements	Engineering	1.00%	3,000,000.00
Denial of Service	2006	2030	Third Party	Other	Non-Elemental	Engineering	0.00%	2,000,000.00
Non-fatal Injuries - Occupant/User	2006	2030	Occupant/User	Other	Non-Elemental	Engineering	0.00%	500,000.00
Non-fatal Injuries - Owner/Manager	2006	2030	Owner/Manager	Other	Non-Elemental	Engineering	0.00%	500,000.00
Non-fatal Injuries - Third Party	2006	2030	Third Party	Other	Non-Elemental	Engineering	0.00%	500,000.00

Event: Cyber Attack (Years 1-10)

Figure 3-18   Event/Outcome Cost Data Summary Page of the Data Report for the Base Case

3.3.2 Results Report

Clicking on the *Results* option under the *Reports* node opens the Results Report. The Results Report consists of these eight sections: (1) a Cover Sheet; (2) Summary of Economic Measures of Performance; (3) Summary of Life-Cycle Costs; (4) Summary of Life-Cycle Costs: Input and Event-Related; (5) Summary of Costs by Alternative sorted by Budget Category (e.g., Cost Item, Bearer, Component, Strategy, and Present Value Dollar Amount); (6) Summary of Annual Costs by Alternative and Budget Category (e.g., Present Value Dollar Amounts for each Year for Capital Investment, O&M, Other, and in Total); (7) Summary of Annual Costs by Alternative (e.g., Present Value Dollar Amounts for each Year for each Alternative); and (8) Summary of Annual and Cumulative Net Savings by Alternative.

Figure 3-19 reproduces the Summary of Economic Measures of Performance page for the case study. This page is included as a convenient summary of all four measures of economic performance—LCC, PVNS, SIR, and AIRR. The measures of economic performance correspond to the drop down menu on the Cost Summary window. It is important to note that if you use the "Copy Alternative" feature (see Section 3.2) to copy the Base Case to another alternative and do not make any changes to input costs and event-related costs, the SIR and AIRR are not defined and hence will not be reported.

Summary of Economic Measures of Performance

Alternative	Economic Measure			
	LCC ($)	PVNS ($)	SIR	AIRR
Base Case	4,642,554	0	—	--
Alternative 1	4,358,912	283,642	1.46	8.63%
Alternative 2	4,254,211	388,343	1.49	8.73%
Alternative 3	4,858,660	-216,106	0.78	5.97%

Figure 3-19   Summary of Economic Measures of Performance Page of the Results Report for the Case Study

Figure 3-20 reproduces the Summary of Life-Cycle Costs Page of the Results Report for the case study. All costs are expressed in present dollar amounts. When you examine Figure 3-20, you will note that it is a reproduction of the Cost Summary window for the baseline analysis. Figure 3-20 includes the check boxes to indicate clearly whether any data elements have been excluded from the life-cycle cost totals. The table in Figure 3-20 is the starting point for the "drill down" analysis of the computed values for life-cycle costs.

Summary of Life-Cycle Costs

		Base Case ($)	Alternative 1 ($)	Alternative 2 ($)	Alternative 3 ($)
	Total Life-Cycle	4,642,554	4,358,912	4,254,211	4,858,660
Bearer:	Owner/Manager	2,727,924	3,025,709	3,186,422	3,412,135
	Occupant/User	1,436,005	1,113,214	850,772	1,232,480
	Third Party	478,625	219,988	217,017	214,045
Category:	Capital Investment	1,149,782	1,765,452	1,934,818	2,152,869
	O&M	2,999,580	2,369,101	2,098,997	2,489,357
	Other	493,192	224,358	220,396	216,434
Component:	Building/Facility	2,361,448	2,639,496	2,888,239	3,809,675
	Building/Facility Site	141,551	234,626	309,626	234,626
	Non-Elemental	2,139,555	1,484,790	1,056,346	814,359
Strategy:	Engineering Alternatives	3,113,247	3,045,065	2,940,364	3,544,813
	Management Practices	1,529,307	1,313,847	1,313,847	1,313,847
	Financial Mechanisms	0	0	0	0

Figure 3-20   Summary of Life-Cycle Costs Page of the Results Report for the Case Study

Figure 3-21 is the first page of the three-page Summary of Life-Cycle Costs: Input and Event-Related portion of the Results Report. All costs are expressed in present dollar amounts and are organized around the Cost summary window with subheadings for Input and Event-Related costs. Reference to Figure 3-21 shows how event-related costs decline going from the Base Case (i.e., minimum acceptable level of performance) to Alternative 3 (i.e., Enhanced Chem/Bio Protection). Reference to Figure 3-21 shows clearly that event-related costs have to be balanced against input costs. For example, the present value input costs for Alternatives 1 and 2 are approximately 5 % greater than the present value of input costs for the Base Case, whereas their event-related costs are about one fourth of the Base Case.

Figure 3-22 is the first page of the two-page Summary of Costs by Alternative portion of the Results Report. Figure 3-22 covers the Base Case. All costs are expressed in present value dollar amounts and include designations for Bearer, Component, and Strategy. The designations map individual cost items into the cost-accounting framework. If you wish to examine how a particular cost item contributes to the amounts shown on the Summary of Life-Cycle Costs page, choose the cost item, see where it fits in the cost-accounting framework, and then trace it back to the Summary of Life-Cycle Costs page. For example, two cost items—Electricity and Site Security—account for three quarters of O&M life-cycle costs. Site Security accounts for all of Management Practices life-cycle costs and slightly more than two thirds of Non-Elemental life-cycle costs.

Summary of Life-Cycle Costs: Input and Event-Related

		Base Case ($)	Alternative 1 ($)	Alternative 2 ($)	Alternative 3 ($)
	Total Life-Cycle	4,642,554	4,358,912	4,254,211	4,858,660
	Input	3,988,596	4,183,096	4,089,267	4,704,589
	Event	653,957	175,816	164,943	154,071
Bearer:	× Owner/Manager	2,727,924	3,025,709	3,186,422	3,412,135
	Input	2,676,930	3,015,266	3,178,432	3,406,597
	Event	50,993	10,443	7,991	5,538
	× Occupant/User	1,436,005	1,113,214	850,772	1,232,480
	Input	1,311,666	1,077,429	820,435	1,207,591
	Event	124,339	35,785	30,337	24,889
	× Third Party	478,625	219,988	217,017	214,045
	Input	0	90,401	90,401	90,401
	Event	478,625	129,587	126,616	123,644
Category:	× Capital Investment	1,149,782	1,765,452	1,934,818	2,152,869
	Input	1,106,072	1,757,194	1,920,360	2,148,526
	Event	43,710	8,258	14,458	4,343
	× O&M	2,999,580	2,369,101	2,098,997	2,489,357
	Input	2,882,525	2,335,501	2,078,507	2,465,663
	Event	117,056	33,600	20,490	23,695

Figure 3-21   Summary of Life-Cycle Costs: Inputs and Event-Related Page of the Results Report for the Case Study

Summary of Costs by Alternative

Base Case: Basic Renovation

Budget Category	Cost Item	Bearer	Component	Strategy	Present Value ($)
Capital Investment					
	Basic Renovation	Owner/Manager	Building/Facility Elements	Engineering Alternative	1,000,000
	Damage to Data Center	Owner/Manager	Building/Facility Elements	Engineering Alternative	5,142
	Damage to Data Center	Owner/Manager	Building/Facility Elements	Engineering Alternative	38,566
	HVAC Upgrade	Owner/Manager	Building/Facility Elements	Engineering Alternative	7,914
	Salvage	Owner/Manager	Building/Facility Elements	Engineering Alternative	-1,942
	Site Protection	Owner/Manager	Building/Facility Site Work	Engineering Alternative	100,000
O&M					
	Business Interruption	Occupant/User	Non-Elemental	Engineering Alternative	58,266
	Business Interruption	Occupant/User	Non-Elemental	Engineering Alternative	14,567
	Duct Cleaning	Occupant/User	Building/Facility Elements	Engineering Alternative	1,583
	Electricity	Occupant/User	Building/Facility Elements	Engineering Alternative	831,024
	HVAC Repairs	Occupant/User	Building/Facility Elements	Engineering Alternative	12,916
	Record Reconstruction	Occupant/User	Non-Elemental	Engineering Alternative	23,150
	Record Reconstruction	Occupant/User	Non-Elemental	Engineering Alternative	21,071
	Site Lighting	Owner/Manager	Building/Facility Site Work	Engineering Alternative	41,551
	Site Security	Owner/Manager	Non-Elemental	Management Practice	1,529,307
	Telecom Services	Occupant/User	Building/Facility Elements	Engineering Alternative	466,143
Other					
	Denial of Service	Third Party	Non-Elemental	Engineering Alternative	5,827
	Denial of Service	Third Party	Non-Elemental	Engineering Alternative	23,307

Figure 3-22   Summary of Costs by Alternative Page of the Results Report for the Base Case

In developing a cost-effective risk mitigation plan, it is useful to see how costs are distributed over time. The Results Report provides two separate means for examining and assessing annual costs. The Summary of Annual Costs by Alternative and Budget Category provides a detailed disaggregated synopsis of annual costs. Thus, if you want to examine how major equipment replacements affect annual costs, examine the entries under the Capital Investment heading and look for years in which significant increases in costs occur. The Summary of Annual Costs by Alternative provides aggregated side-by-side comparisons of the alternatives being evaluated. Figure 3-23 reproduces the Summary of Annual Costs by Alternative page for the data center case study. These side-by-side comparisons are useful in determining when a particular alternative has a "bulge" in costs—say at the beginning of the study period or associated with a major replacement—or when one alternative's annual costs begin to escalate at a significantly higher rate. Both pieces of information are useful in understanding the pros and cons of each alternative being evaluated. It is important to recognize that the goal of the analysis is to gain insights into the decision-making process.

In addition to seeing how costs are distributed over time, it is useful to see how net savings accumulate over time. The Summary of Annual and Cumulative Net Savings by Alternative provides net savings computations vis-à-vis the Base Case for each Alternative analyzed. Figure 3-24 reproduces the Summary of Annual and Cumulative Net Savings by Alternative page for the Enhanced Security alternative for the data center case study. This set of calculations provides a measure of how long it takes an alternative to generate enough net savings to break even vis-à-vis the Base Case.

Year	Base Case	Alternative 1	Alternative 2	Alternative 3
		Summary of Annual Costs by Alternative		
		Present Value ($)		
2006	1,369,354	1,990,797	2,135,016	2,448,389
2007	252,245	225,431	201,895	196,692
2008	236,225	170,232	148,227	143,351
2009	225,039	159,437	146,646	219,904
2010	207,178	149,328	130,092	125,812
2011	194,025	143,859	126,874	122,863
2012	181,708	130,995	120,629	181,359
2013	173,085	122,692	106,972	103,450
2014	159,375	114,917	100,219	96,919
2015	149,262	107,635	99,236	149,579
2016	150,243	104,212	91,364	88,467
2017	142,911	100,267	88,920	86,206
2018	131,747	91,413	84,610	126,343
2019	123,373	85,617	75,117	72,734
2020	115,532	80,189	70,372	68,139
2021	109,884	75,106	69,596	104,191
2022	110,813	82,217	76,801	78,007
2023	94,879	67,662	60,083	58,246
2024	88,851	61,712	57,250	85,929
2025	84,500	57,802	50,788	49,176
2026	77,923	54,140	47,583	46,072
2027	72,975	50,710	47,098	70,872
2028	68,341	47,498	41,766	40,440
2029	64,988	45,673	40,610	39,367
2030	58,097	39,370	36,446	56,154

Figure 3-23   **Summary of Annual Costs by Alternative Page of the Results Report for the Data Center Case Study**

Summary of Annual and Cumulative Net Savings by Alternative

Alternative 1: Proposed Alternative -- Enhanced Security

Year	Present Value ($)	Annual Net Savings	Cumulative Net Savings
2006	1,990,797	-621,443	-621,443
2007	225,431	26,814	-594,629
2008	170,232	65,993	-528,636
2009	159,437	65,602	-463,034
2010	149,328	57,850	-405,185
2011	143,859	50,166	-355,019
2012	130,995	50,713	-304,306
2013	122,692	50,393	-253,913
2014	114,917	44,458	-209,455
2015	107,635	41,627	-167,828
2016	104,212	46,032	-121,796
2017	100,267	42,645	-79,152
2018	91,413	40,334	-38,818
2019	85,617	37,756	-1,062
2020	80,189	35,343	34,281
2021	75,106	34,778	69,059
2022	82,217	28,596	97,655
2023	67,662	27,216	124,871
2024	61,712	27,139	152,010
2025	57,802	26,698	178,708
2026	54,140	23,783	202,492
2027	50,710	22,265	224,756
2028	47,498	20,843	245,599
2029	45,673	19,315	264,915
2030	39,370	18,727	283,642

Figure 3-24   Summary of Annual and Cumulative Net Savings by Alternative Page of the Results Report for the Data Center Case Study

3.4   Project Notebook

Clicking the *Notebook* option under the *Reports* node opens the Project Notebook Report. The Project Notebook Report consists of these five sections: (1) a Cover Sheet; (2) Project-Related Notes; (3) Alternative-Related Notes; (4) Input Cost-Related Notes; and (5) Event/Outcome Cost-Related Notes.

The purpose of the Project Notebook Report is to provide a means for documenting the sources of key data elements. The sections of the Project Notebook Report are designed promote documentation in-depth. At the highest level it provides project-related notes. These notes are entered via the Notebook Icon in the Project Description window. Clicking the Notebook Icon opens a dialog box that allows you to enter text, numerical data, or other reference material. The type of material appearing in the Project-Related Notes section includes but is not limited to information on how the risk assessment was performed, key assets[13] requiring protection, vulnerabilities[14] documented, key contact persons involved in the risk assessment, the title of the risk assessment document, and how to obtain a printed or electronic copy of the document.

Material contained in the Alternative-Related Notes section describes how information from the risk assessment was used to formulate the alternative. This includes how the combinations of mitigation strategies—engineering, management, and financial—were packaged and how that combination addresses vulnerabilities identified in the risk assessment.

Material contained in the Input Cost-Related Notes section describes for each cost item the sources of cost estimates. Material contained in this section on Capital Cost items covers the timing of their occurrence and whether or not they will require replacement and, if so, at what frequency. Material contained in this section on O&M and Other cost items covers the timing and frequency of their occurrence.

Material contained in the Event/Outcome Cost-Related Notes section describes for an event/outcome cost item how the consequence[15] of it occurring was estimated. The consequence of an event-outcome combination on an asset is generally estimated as the amount of loss or damage that can be expected from that combination.

3.5 Online Help

The Cost-Effectiveness Tool contains two on-line help features: (1) a Software Tips screen that highlights important software attributes and (2) an on-line version of this Users Manual. Open the Help window by clicking *CET Help* from the Help menu or by pressing the F1 function key.

Figure 3-25 shows the basic Help tree and the Software Tips screen. The Help tree appears on the left-hand side of the figure. It contains three nodes—*Welcome, Software Tips* and *Users Manual*. Only the *Users Manual* node contains lower-level nodes. These

---

[13] An asset is any constructed facility, its contents (physical systems, information, and personnel), or activities (functions) that have positive value to an owner or society as a whole.
[14] A vulnerability is any weakness in an asset's design, implementation, or operation that can result in damage to the asset. Such weaknesses can occur in facility characteristics, equipment properties, personnel behavior, locations of people and equipment, or operational and personnel practices.
[15] A consequence is the immediate, short-, and long-term effects of an event-outcome combination. Some examples of relevant consequences include: public or asset personnel (e.g., occupants, users, or third parties) fatalities or injuries, property damage or loss, disruption of public or private operations, environmental damage, and loss of critical data.

lower-level nodes correspond to the section and subsection headings of this report. The right-hand side of Figure 3-25 lists six important software tips. The Software Tips screen is designed as a handy reference for first-time users. It highlights material contained in this report as well as several basic concepts for navigating within the software and for saving results.

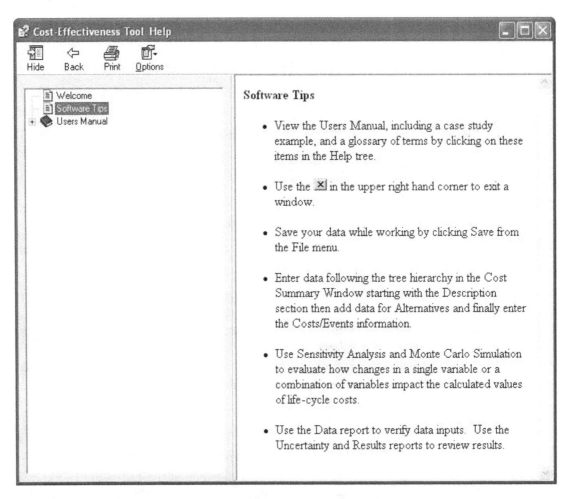

Figure 3-25   Cost-Effectiveness Tool Help Window, Help Tree, and Software Tips

Clicking the lower-level *Software Glossary* node opens a glossary of terms. The glossary of terms corresponds to Appendix B of this report. The terms are arranged in alphabetical order. The glossary contains over 80 terms. Each term is listed in bold followed by its definition. Associated with most terms are a Notes section and an Example section. The Notes section lists the output windows, input windows, and reports which contain that term. The Notes section also includes a link to key sections and subsections of this report, where additional information on the term of interest is given. Whenever appropriate, an example is given. The purpose of the Example section is to link the term to the data center case study contained in the ***Data Center Case Study.lcc*** file.

4   Treatment of Uncertainty and Risk

Decision makers typically experience uncertainty about the correct values to use in establishing basic assumptions and in estimating future costs. Investments in long-lived projects, such as the erection of new constructed facilities or additions and alterations to existing constructed facilities, are characterized by uncertainties regarding project life, operation and maintenance costs, revenues, and other factors that affect project economics. Since future values of these variable factors are generally unknown, it is difficult to make reliable economic evaluations.

The traditional approach to uncertainty in project investment analysis is to apply economic methods of project evaluation to best-guess estimates of project input variables, as if they were certain estimates, and then to present results in a single-value, deterministic fashion. When projects are evaluated without regard to uncertainty of inputs to the analysis, decision makers may have insufficient information to measure and evaluate the financial risk of investing in a project having a different outcome from what is expected. ASTM Standard Guide E 1369 surveys six widely used techniques for treating uncertainty and financial risk in the economic evaluation of constructed facilities.[16] A subset of these techniques is implemented within CET 4.0.

CET 4.0 addresses uncertainty and financial risk in a structured, three-part manner. First, best-guess estimates are used to establish a baseline analysis. The baseline analysis uses fixed parameter values to calculate economic measures of performance. The results of the baseline analysis allow the alternative combinations of risk mitigation strategies to be ranked according to their economic measures of performance. The ranking of the alternatives and the calculated measures of performance provide a frame of reference for the treatment of uncertainty and financial risk. Second, a sensitivity analysis is performed in which selected inputs are varied about their baseline values. The sensitivity analysis is especially helpful in identifying shifts in the rank ordering of alternatives. The sensitivity analysis, although it addresses uncertainty in input values, produces only a crude measure of financial risk. Third, a Monte Carlo simulation is performed to obtain an explicit measure of financial risk associated with the competing alternatives. Monte Carlo simulation is especially useful in identifying shifts in the rank ordering of alternatives and documenting the factors and circumstances associated with those shifts. This section extends the guided tour by laying out a systematic approach to the treatment of uncertainty and risk

4.1   Perform Sensitivity Analysis

Recall that in the baseline analysis all data elements entering into the calculations are fixed. The baseline analysis includes both input costs and event-related costs. Thus, the baseline analysis is a complete analysis in all respects but one; it does not address the effects of uncertainty. For example, although the baseline analysis includes event-related

---

[16] ASTM International. "Standard Guide for Selecting Techniques for Treating Uncertainty and Risk in the Economic Evaluation of Buildings and Building Systems," E 1369, *Annual Book of ASTM Standards: 2006*. Vol. 04.11. West Conshohocken, PA: ASTM International.

information, the probabilities and costs of any event-related outcomes are fixed. Whereas these probabilities and costs are estimated based on the best available data, there is uncertainty associated with them.

Sensitivity analysis, as implemented in Version 4.0, addresses uncertainty by letting you evaluate how changes in: (1) a single variable impacts the calculated values of life-cycle costs and (2) multiple variables impact the calculated values of life-cycle costs. Depending on the variable (variables) selected, it (they) may impact a single alternative or it (they) may impact all alternatives.

The Sensitivity Analysis window is entered by clicking the *Sensitivity* option under the *Uncertainty* node. The window, as configured in Version 4.0, has three tabs: (1) Change in a Single Factor; (2) Most Significant Factors; and (3) Change in Multiple Factors.

4.1.1   Change in a Single Factor Tab

The left-hand side of the Change in a Single Factor tab lists the hierarchy of factors available for evaluation. Each factor is associated with a node in the hierarchy. Upon entering the tab, the Project and Alternatives nodes appear at the left. All alternatives evaluated in the baseline analysis are listed immediately below the Alternatives node. The squares immediately to the left of each node in the hierarchy are marked with a + (plus sign) or a – (minus sign). A plus sign means that additional nodes and/or factors reside beneath that node. A minus sign means that a node has been opened. Since each project has alternatives associated with it, upon entering the Change in a Single Factor tab, you will note that the Alternatives node has a minus sign in its square on the left.

Nodes can be opened or closed. For example clicking the square by the Project node opens the node and the single factor Discount Rate (7.00 %) appears beneath it. Note that there is no square to the left of Discount Rate. This means that Discount Rate is a factor which can be selected for evaluation. Note that the factor line in the hierarchy includes both the factor name (Discount Rate) and its value (7.00 %). Highlighting the factor Discount Rate (7.00 %) selects that factor. The right-hand side of the screen includes the Results group box, a drop down menu for percent changes about the baseline value of the selected factor, and a *Compute* button. Clicking on the *Compute* button causes three sets of life-cycle cost values to be computed. Figure 4-1 shows the results of a 10 % deviation about the baseline value of the discount rate. Note that the name of the factor appears at the upper left-hand corner of the Results group box. Since the discount rate is the same for each alternative, results for both the Base Case and the Proposed Alternatives are reported. Note that the Minimum, Baseline, and Maximum values for the factor, Discount Rate, are displayed. Reference to Figure 4-1 shows that the discount rate has a fairly strong impact on the computed value of life-cycle costs for both the Base Case and the Proposed Alternatives. While the range of values was fairly wide, in each case Alternative 1 emerged as the cost-effective risk mitigation plan.

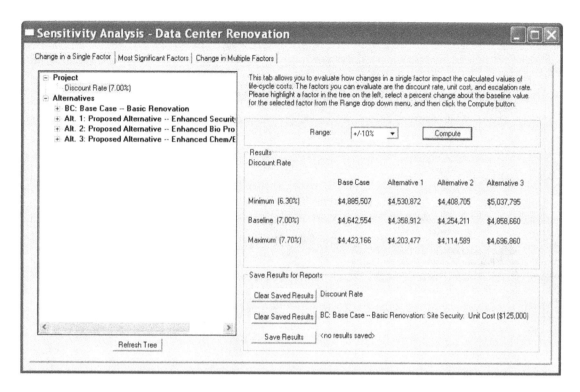

Figure 4-1 **Sensitivity Analysis Window: Using the Change in a Single Factor Tab to Evaluate the Impact of the Discount Rate on Life-Cycle Costs**

Figure 4-2 uses the Base Case to illustrate how to open up the hierarchy within a given alternative. The nodes immediately beneath the BC: Basic Renovation node are labeled Costs and Events. Additional nodes are listed beneath the Costs and Events nodes. Opening the Costs node, we see that 10 nodes are listed beneath it. These nodes correspond to the cost items entered via the Capital Investment, O&M, and Other Cost Information windows. Note that each of the 10 nodes indicates the budget category it falls under. One of the 10 nodes has been opened—O&M: Site Security—to reveal its factors. The factor selected for analysis is the Unit Cost of Site Security. Under the Range drop down menu, we have selected a 10 % deviation about the baseline value of the annually recurring Unit Cost of $125 000. Clicking the *Compute* button causes three sets of values to be computed. Because this factor only affects the Base Case, only values for the Base Case are displayed. Reference to the Results group box reveals that this factor has a strong impact on life-cycle costs.

Event-related costs are evaluated by opening the Events node for the alternative of interest. The nodes listed beneath the Events node are the individual events defined and used in the case study: CBRE Attack, Cyber Attack (Years 1-10), and Cyber Attack (Years 11-25). Beneath each event node are the outcomes. If an outcome had costs associated with it, then the event/outcome cost items are listed as nodes beneath it. The factors—unit cost and escalation rate—appear beneath each event/outcome cost item.

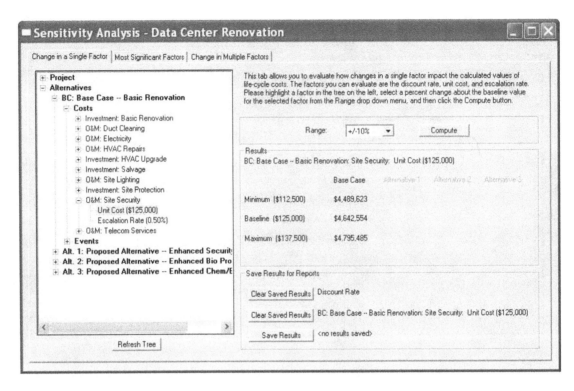

Figure 4-2   Sensitivity Analysis Window: Using the Change in a Single Factor Tab to Evaluate the Impact of the Unit Cost of Site Security on Life-Cycle Costs for the Base Case

The bottom right-hand portion of the window contains the Save Results for Reports group box. As its name suggests, the *Save Results* buttons may be used to save up to three sets of computed results. For example, both the discount rate and the annually recurring costs for site security have a strong impact on life-cycle costs. Thus, saving these results might be useful in supporting a recommendation for Alternative 1 (Enhanced Security) or Alternative 2 (Enhanced Bio Protection). Any results that you choose to save will appear in the Uncertainty Report.

4.1.2   Most Significant Factors Tab

The Most Significant Factors tab allows you to identify those factors which have the greatest impact on life-cycle costs. Clicking the *Compute* button causes the discount rate, each unit cost, and each escalation rate to be varied by +10 % and −10 %, while holding all other input variables at their baseline values. A table is then generated listing each factor and the associated change in life-cycle cost. The factor having the greatest impact on life-cycle cost is listed first. All other factors are listed in descending order of their impact on life-cycle cost. Figure 4-3 illustrates the output from the Most Significant Factors tab. It is important to note that a *10 % decrease* in a factor may result in an *increase* in life-cycle costs and a *10 % increase* in a factor may result in a *decrease* in life-cycle costs.

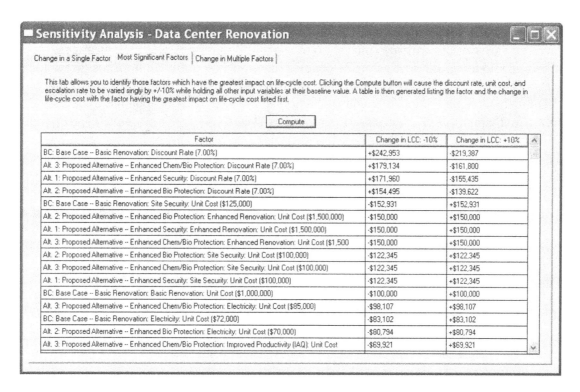

Figure 4-3   **Sensitivity Analysis Window: Using the Most Significant Factors Tab to Evaluate the Impact of +/-10 % Changes of Each Factor on Life-Cycle Costs for the Case Study**

4.1.3   Change in Multiple Factors Tab

The Change in Multiple Factors tab allows you to evaluate how combinations of factors impact the calculated values of life-cycle costs. The Change in Multiple Factors tab is designed to be used in conjunction with the Most Significant Factors tab. Use the Most Significant Factors tab to identify candidates for inclusion in the Change in Multiple Factors portion of the sensitivity analysis. For example, you might want to focus on those factors that have the greatest impact on life-cycle costs. The Change in Multiple Factors tab is designed to set ranges on how the combinations of factors affect life-cycle costs by using a "best case" and "worst case" setting for each factor selected. The best case and worst case settings are drawn from the minus signs (best case) and plus signs (worst case) that appear in the Most Significant Factors tab. Recall that values appearing on the Most Significant Factors tab are based on a 10 % deviation about the baseline value. The Change in Multiple Factors tab allows users to specify a range of deviations about the baseline value for the factor of interest. Thus, although a 10 % deviation is permissible, other values for the deviation are also permissible.

The left-hand side of the Change in Multiple Factors tab lists the hierarchy of factors that can be included in this portion of the sensitivity analysis. Each factor is associated with a node in the hierarchy. Upon entering the tab, the Project and Alternatives nodes appear at the left. All alternatives evaluated in the baseline analysis are listed immediately below the Alternatives node. The squares immediately to the left of each node in the hierarchy are marked with a + (plus sign) or a − (minus sign). A plus sign means that additional nodes and/or factors reside beneath that node. A minus sign means that a node has been opened. Since each project has alternatives associated with it, upon entering the Change in Multiple Factors tab, you will note that the Alternatives node has a minus sign in its square on the left. Nodes can be opened or closed.

Figure 4-4 illustrates how to open up the hierarchy and select factors for analysis. The discount rate node has been opened and a range of +/- 25 % about the baseline value has been selected. The Discount Rate will be included in the analysis, since the *Include Factor* box has been checked. The nodes immediately beneath the BC: Basic Renovation node are labeled Costs and Events have also been opened. These nodes correspond to the cost items entered via the Capital Investment, O&M, and Other Cost Information windows. Note that each of the 10 nodes indicates the budget category it falls under. One of the 10 nodes has been opened—O&M: Site Security—to reveal factors. The factor to be selected for inclusion in the analysis is the Unit Cost of Site Security. Nine other factors were also selected for inclusion in the analysis: (1) the Unit Cost of the Basic Renovation; (2-4) the Unit Cost of the Enhanced Renovation for Alternatives 1, 2, and 3; (5-7) the Unit Cost of Site Security for Alternatives 1, 2, and 3; and (8-9) the Unit Cost of Improved Productivity (IAQ) for Alternatives 2 and 3.

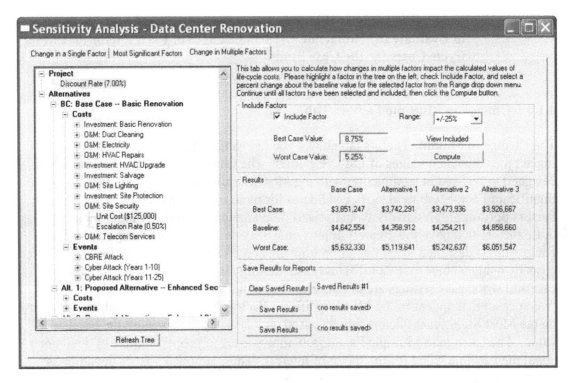

Figure 4-4   Sensitivity Analysis Window: Using the Change in Multiple Factors Tab to Evaluate the Impact of Combinations of Factors on Life-Cycle Costs for the Case Study

Because the Change in Multiple Factors tab allows combinations of factors to be analyzed, an Included Multiple Factors window was developed. Figure 4-5 lists the eleven factors included in the analysis and their range of values, expressed as a +/- % deviation from the baseline value.

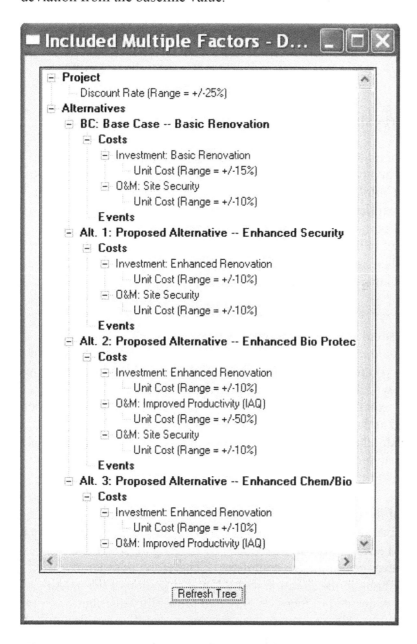

Figure 4-5   Sensitivity Analysis Window: Tree Structure Showing Combinations of Factors Included in the Sensitivity Analysis

Returning to Figure 4-4, we see that clicking the *Compute* button causes three sets of values to be computed. The calculated values for life-cycle costs correspond to each factor being set at its best-case value, baseline value, and worst-case value. Reference to

Figure 4-4 shows that this combination of factors has a strong impact on the computed values of life-cycle costs for both the Base Case and the Proposed Alternatives. While the range of values was fairly wide, in each case Alternative 2, Enhanced Bio Protection, emerged as the cost-effective risk mitigation plan.

The bottom right-hand portion of the window contains the Save Results for Reports group box. As its name suggests, the *Save Results* buttons may be used to save up to three sets of computed results. Any results that you choose to save will appear in the Uncertainty Report.

4.2   Perform Monte Carlo Simulation

Monte Carlo simulation, as implemented in Version 4.0, allows you to evaluate how changes in a single variable or a combination of variables impact the calculated values of life-cycle cost. The Monte Carlo simulation feature is designed to address two analysis needs. First, it provides an explicit measure of financial risk—the probability of investing in a project whose economic outcome is different from what is desired or expected. Second, it is useful in identifying shifts in the rank ordering of alternatives and documenting the factors and circumstances associated with these shifts. The Monte Carlo Simulation window is entered by clicking the *Monte Carlo* option under the *Uncertainty* node.

Setting up the Monte Carlo simulation involves the specification of an experimental design. Use information provided in the Most Significant Factors tab and the Change in Multiple Factors tab to help you formulate the experimental design. Those tabs help you choose which variables you wish to select for in-depth analysis. Those tabs are useful because specification of the experimental design is a two-step process: (1) defining which variables are to be simulated and (2) selecting the number of simulations. Within Version 4.0, the number of simulations is set at 1 000 to ensure that values in the tails of the distribution for each variable of interest would be selected for inclusion in the analysis.

In reality, the exact nature of the parent probability distribution for each variable is unknown. Estimates of the parameters (e.g., mean and variance) of the parent probability distribution can be made and uncertainty can be reduced by investigation and research. However, uncertainty can never be eliminated completely. Therefore, in order to implement the procedure without undue attention to the characterization of the parent probability distribution, it was decided to focus on only two probability distributions: (1) the triangular and (2) the uniform. One reason for using these probability distributions is that they are both defined over a finite interval. They are also used frequently in cost-risk analyses.[17] Furthermore, the specification of each probability distribution is accomplished with as few as two data points. The triangular distribution is widely used in simulation modeling; its specification requires three data points, the minimum value, the most likely value, and the maximum value. The triangular distribution is used

---

[17] ASTM International. "Standard Practice for Measuring Cost Risk of Buildings and Building Systems." E 1946. *Annual Book of ASTM Standards: 2006*. Vol. 04.12. West Conshohocken, PA: ASTM International.

whenever the range of input values is continuous and a clustering about some central value is expected. The uniform distribution is also widely used in simulation modeling; its specification requires only two data points, the minimum value and the maximum value. In addition, all values between the minimum and maximum are equally likely. The uniform distribution is used whenever the range of input values is continuous but no *a priori* reason can be given for expecting clustering about some central value.

4.2.1 Setting up the Simulation and Saving the Results

The Monte Carlo Simulation window is designed to be used in conjunction with the Most Significant Factors tab and the Change in Multiple Factors tab. Use the Most Significant Factors tab to identify candidates for inclusion in the Change in Multiple Factors portion of the sensitivity analysis. Use the Change in Multiple Factors tab to establish likely values for the range of life-cycle cost for a combination of input variables. Once you have established the range (e.g., "best case" and "worst case" values for the combination), the Monte Carlo Simulation window allows you to "fill in" the intermediate values and identify any cases where rank reversals occur.

The left-hand side of the Monte Carlo Simulation window lists the hierarchy of factors that can be included in this portion of the sensitivity analysis. Each factor is associated with a node in the hierarchy. Upon entering the Monte Carlo Simulation window, the Project and Alternatives nodes appear at the left. All alternatives evaluated in the baseline analysis are listed immediately below the Alternatives node. The squares immediately to the left of each node in the hierarchy are marked with a + (plus sign) or a – (minus sign). A plus sign means that additional nodes and/or factors reside beneath that node. A minus sign means that a node has been opened. Since each project has alternatives associated with it, upon entering the Monte Carlo Simulation window, you will note that the Alternatives node has a minus sign in its square on the left. Nodes can be opened or closed.

Because baseline values have already been entered for each factor, the specification of the uniform distribution only requires one data point, while the specification of the triangular distribution requires two data points. Specification of the uniform distribution only requires one data point because it is symmetric about the baseline value. Thus, if a lower bound of 4 % is entered (i.e., the baseline value minus 3 %), the upper bound is calculated automatically as 10 % (i.e., the baseline value plus 3 %). The triangular distribution requires two data points—the lower bound and the upper bound—because the baseline value is used as the most likely value. Note that CET 4.0 imposes two constraints in specifying the triangular distribution (1) the lower bound must be less than the baseline value and (2) the upper bound must be greater than the baseline value.

Figure 4-6 illustrates how to open up the hierarchy and select factors for analysis. The discount rate node has been opened and a probability distribution and a range of values about the baseline value have been selected. In this case the uniform distribution has been selected and a minimum value of 4.00 % has been entered. The maximum value of 10.00 % is calculated automatically based on the symmetric nature of the uniform distribution. The Discount Rate will be included in the analysis, since the *Include Factor* box has been checked.

Ten other factors are included in the Monte Carlo simulation. Two are specific to the Base Case (1) the Unit Cost of the Basic Renovation and (2) the Unit Cost of Site Security; two are specific to Alternative 1 (1) the Unit Cost of the Enhanced Renovation and (2) the Unit Cost of Site Security; three are specific to Alternative 2 (1) the Unit Cost of the Enhanced Renovation, (2) the Unit Cost of Site Security, and (3) the Unit Cost of Improved Productivity (IAQ); and three are specific to Alternative 3 (1) the Unit Cost of the Enhanced Renovation, (2) the Unit Cost of Site Security, and (3) the Unit Cost of Improved Productivity (IAQ). Variations in the values of all ten factors are modeled using a triangular distribution. In each case, the distribution is positively skewed, indicating that the upper tail is longer than the lower tail. This formulation is common in construction and O&M cost estimating, reflecting the potential that cost can increase rapidly. For example, the baseline value for the Unit Cost of Site Security for the Base Case is $125 000 per year. In the Monte Carlo simulation, we have set the lower bound at $110 000 (i.e., the baseline value minus $10 000) and the upper bound at $145 000 (i.e., the baseline value plus $20 000).

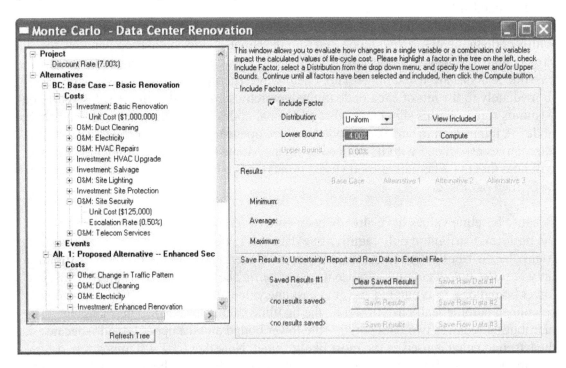

Figure 4-6   Monte Carlo Simulation Window: Using the Monte Carlo Simulation Window to Evaluate the Impact of Combinations of Factors on Life-Cycle Costs for the Case Study

Because the Monte Carlo Simulation window allows combinations of factors to be analyzed, an Included Monte Carlo Factors window was developed. Figure 4-7 lists the eleven factors included in the analysis. For each factor, the window records the associated probability distribution.

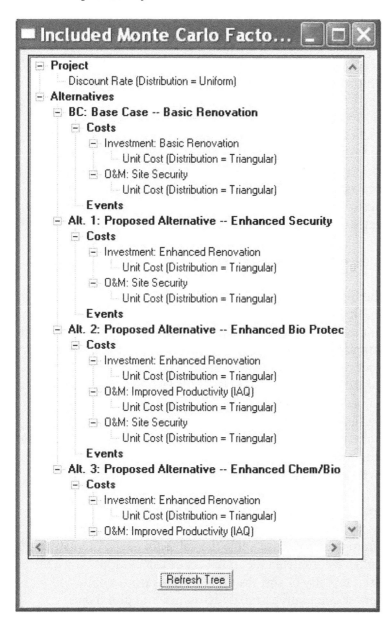

Figure 4-7   Monte Carlo Simulation Window: Tree Structure Showing Combinations of Factors Included in the Monte Carlo Simulation

Returning to Figure 4-6, we see that clicking the *Compute* button causes three sets of values to be computed. The calculated values for life-cycle costs correspond to Minimum, Average, and Maximum values of life-cycle costs observed in the Monte Carlo simulation. Reference to Figure 4-6 shows that this combination of factors has a strong impact on the computed values of life-cycle costs for both the Base Case and the

Proposed Alternatives. While the range of values was fairly wide, in each case Alternative 2, Enhanced Bio Protection, emerged as the cost-effective risk mitigation plan.

The bottom right-hand portion of the window contains the Save Results to Uncertainty Report and Raw Data to External Files group box. As its name suggests, the *Save Results* buttons may be used to save up to three sets of computed results. Any results that you choose to save will appear in the Uncertainty Report. The bottom right-hand portion of the window also contains an option to *Save Raw Data* to an external file. This option allows you to save up to three sets of raw data. If this option is selected, a file for each alternative analyzed (e.g., Base Case, Alternative 1, Alternative 2, and Alternative 3) is saved in the Simulation Data directory under the CET 4.0 directory. Each file is saved in a spreadsheet format. Each file has a *csv* extension. These files are designed so that users can calculate a wide variety of summary statistics and sort and plot the cumulative distribution function of life-cycle cost for each alternative analyzed.

4.2.2   How to Create Customized Charts and Tables

Should you choose to access the files created via the *Save Raw Data* to an external file option, we recommend that you first create an Excel file to retrieve the saved raw data. We recommend that you have at least four worksheets in addition to a worksheet for each alternative analyzed. The additional worksheets are useful in setting up the calculations, summary statistics, and charts for each measure of economic performance (i.e., LCC, PVNS, SIR, and AIRR). All of the information needed to calculate each measure of economic performance is contained in the raw data files. For example, if you wish to create a cumulative distribution function for life-cycle costs, you will need to paste the life-cycle cost values for each alternative into a worksheet, sort each set of values, and set up a placeholder for cumulative probability (i.e., 0.001, 0.002, ..., 0.999, 1.000). Graphing features of Excel can then be used to create a multi-trace plot of the alternatives' life-cycle costs. If other measures of economic performance are desired, use the formulas given in Appendix A to calculate the measure. For example, if summary statistics and charts for the present value of net savings are desired, start with the sorted life-cycle values and subtract from the Base Case value the value for each Alternative (see Equation A.11). Once you have completed the initial set of calculations, you can either generate summary statistics directly or sort the PVNS values from smallest to largest and set up a place holder for cumulative probability in order to plot them.

The *Save Raw Data* to an external file option provides an opportunity to produce customized charts and tables that complement the Monte Carlo simulation material presented in the Uncertainty Report. Figures 4-8 and 4-9 and Table 4-1 are based on the raw data; they record the graphical and tabular results when all eleven factors are varied in combination. The two figures were constructed by first sorting the values of each economic measure from smallest to largest. The resultant cumulative distribution was then plotted. In each figure, the vertical axis records the probability that the economic measure is less than or equal to a specified value. The values recorded on the horizontal axis cover the range of values encountered during the Monte Carlo simulation.

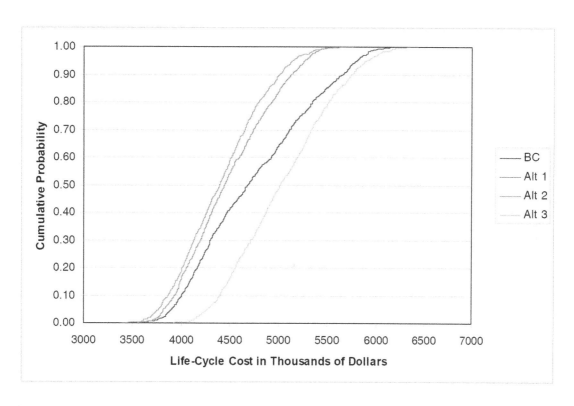

Figure 4-8 **Life-Cycle Costs for the Base Case and the Proposed Alternative in Thousands of Dollars Due to Changes in Five Factors**

Figure 4-8 shows how the life-cycle costs of the Base Case compare to those of the Proposed Alternatives when all eleven factors are varied in combination. In Figure 4-8, life-cycle costs are expressed in thousands of dollars ($K). In analyzing Figure 4-8, it is useful to keep in mind that the values of life-cycle costs for the Base Case and the Proposed Alternatives from the baseline analysis were $4 643K, $4 359K, $4 254K, and $4 859K, respectively. Comparisons between Figure 4-8 and saved results tabulated in the Uncertainty Report (see Figure 4-13) are also helpful in interpreting the results of the Monte Carlo simulation. First, notice that the life-cycle cost trace of Alternatives 1 and 2 in Figure 4-8 always remains to the left of the life-cycle cost trace for the Base Case. Thus, for any given probability (e.g., 0.50, as measured by the 50th percentile recorded in the Uncertainty Report (see Figure 4-13)), the life-cycle cost of the Alternative 2 ($4 396K) is less than the life-cycle cost of the Base Case ($4 687K). Similarly, for any given life-cycle cost (e.g., $4 500K), the probability of being less than or equal to that cost is higher for Alternative 2 (0.59) than for the Base Case (0.42). Second, the horizontal distance between the Alternative 2 and the Base Case gets larger as the cumulative probability moves from 0.00 to 1.00. This translates into a wider range of life-cycle costs for the Base Case (i.e., maximum minus minimum); it is reflected in the higher standard deviation for the Base Case recorded in the last column of the statistical measure section of the Uncertainty Report (see Figure 4-13). Figure 4-8 demonstrates that Alternative 2 is the most cost-effective risk mitigation plan. However, it is instructive to examine how the use of other economic measures sheds light on other aspects of its cost-effectiveness.

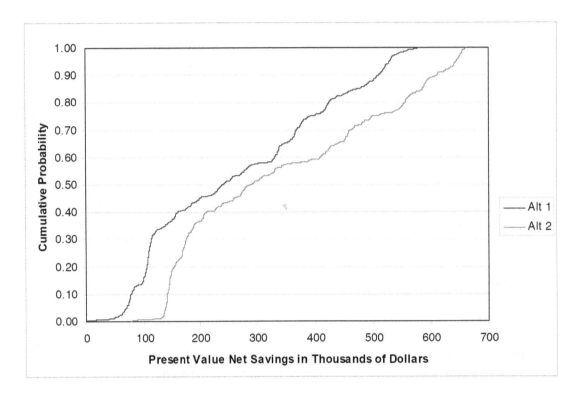

Figure 4-9   Present Value Net Savings in Thousands of Dollars for the Proposed Alternative Due to Changes in Five Factors

Figure 4-9 shows how present value net savings (PVNS) of Alternatives 1 and 2 vary when all eleven factors are varied in combination. In analyzing Figure 4-9, it is useful to keep in mind that the value of PVNS resulting from the baseline analysis was $388K for Alternative 2 and $284K for Alternative 1. Turning now to Figure 4-9, we see that a value of PVNS equal to $200K occurs at 0.37 on the cumulative distribution function for Alternative 2. Stated another way, there is a probability of 0.63 that PVNS of Alternative 2 will exceed $200K. Reference to Figure 4-9 reveals that PVNS of Alternative 2 exceeds $400K for approximately 40 % of the observations resulting from the Monte Carlo simulation.

Table 4-1 summarizes the results of the Monte Carlo simulation for the Proposed Alternatives. Four economic measures are reported. The values of life-cycle costs (LCC) and present value net savings (PVNS) are reported in thousands of dollars ($K). This facilitates comparisons between the values in the table and the information plotted in Figures 4-8 and 4-9. A PVNS greater than zero indicates a cost-effective risk mitigation plan. The savings-to-investment ratio (SIR) is a dimensionless number. An SIR greater than 1.0 indicates a cost-effective risk mitigation plan. The adjusted internal rate of return (AIRR) is expressed as an annual percentage rate. An AIRR greater than the baseline value for the discount rate of 7 % indicates a cost-effective risk mitigation plan. Reference to Table 4-1 reveals the superior performance 0f Alternative 2 – Enhanced Bio Protection. Reference to Table 4-1 reveals that the minimum values for PVNS, SIR, and AIRR indicate marginal performance of Alternative 1 vis-à-vis the Base Case. An examination of the raw data, however, reveals that marginal performance is associated with a single observation. Values in the inter-quartile range (i.e., the middle 50 % of the observations) support Alternative 2 as the most cost-effective risk mitigation plan.

Table 4-1   Summary Statistics for the Proposed Alternative Due to Changes in Five Factors

Economic Measure	Statistical Measure						
	Minimum	25%	50%	75%	Maximum	Mean	Standard Deviation
LCC_{BC}	3614	4240	4687	5226	6171	4755	605
$LCC_{Alt\,1}$	3549	4136	4447	4832	5600	4492	447
$PVNS_{Alt\,1}$	-5	108	239	394	587	264	160
$SIR_{Alt\,1}$	0.991	1.170	1.358	1.596	2.774	1.414	0.278
$AIRR_{Alt\,1}$	0.060	0.077	0.084	0.093	0.107	0.085	0.010
$LCC_{Alt\,2}$	3385	4069	4396	4720	5759	4415	430
$PVNS_{Alt\,2}$	77	168	291	498	662	340	182
$SIR_{Alt\,2}$	1.092	1.206	1.355	1.594	2.671	1.417	0.238
$AIRR_{Alt\,2}$	0.054	0.075	0.083	0.093	0.111	0.084	0.012
$LCC_{Alt\,3}$	3922	4635	5019	5430	6430	5049	506
$PVNS_{Alt\,3}$	-434	-390	-332	-206	-77	-293	108
$SIR_{Alt\,3}$	0.284	0.624	0.699	0.815	0.945	0.713	0.122
$AIRR_{Alt\,3}$	0.008	0.042	0.051	0.064	0.086	0.053	0.014

4.3   Use and Interpretation of the Uncertainty Report

Clicking on the *Uncertainty* option under the *Reports* node opens the Uncertainty Report. The Uncertainty Report consists of these five sections: (1) a Cover Sheet; (2) any sensitivity analyses saved under the Change in a Single Factor tab; (3) if computed, the rank-ordered factors and their associated values from the Most Significant Factors tab; (4) any sensitivity analyses saved under the Change in Multiple Factors tab; and (5) any Monte Carlo simulations saved.

Figure 4-10 presents a saved sensitivity analysis from the Change in a Single Factor tab for a plus or minus 10 % change in the discount rate. Figure 4-10 largely reproduces the Results section from the Change in a Single Factor tab (see Figure 4-1). Figure 4-10 records the factor name in the upper left-hand corner along with the range for which life-cycle costs are calculated (i.e., the Minimum, Baseline, and Maximum values of that factor). Note that more than one range can be used and saved for a single factor. For example, if you wanted to see how lowering the discount rate to 5.25 % or raising it to 8.75 % would affect the calculated values for life-cycle costs, you would use the +/-25 % change from the drop down Range box in the Change in a Single Factor tab to *Compute* the values and *Save Results* for the Uncertainty Report.

| | | Change in a Single Factor | | |
		Saved Results #1		
Discount Rate				
Range: +/-10%				
	Base Case	Alternative 1	Alternative 2	Alternative 3
Minimum (6.30%)	$4,885,507	$4,530,872	$4,408,705	$5,037,795
Baseline (7.00%)	$4,642,554	$4,358,912	$4,254,211	$4,858,660
Maximum (7.70%)	$4,423,166	$4,203,477	$4,114,589	$4,696,860

Figure 4-10   Saved Sensitivity Analysis Page of the Uncertainty Report for a +/-10 % Change in the Discount Rate

Figure 4-11 presents the first page of the rank-ordered factors and their associated values from the Most Significant Factors tab. Note that reductions in the discount rate for both the Base Case and the Proposed Alternatives result in increases in life-cycle costs. The rank ordering of the factors provides a convenient means for identifying those factors which merit closer examination via either the Change in a Single Factor tab or the Change in Multiple Factors tab. Although all factors are varied by plus or minus 10 % in the Most Significant Factors tab, you can use the Change in a Single Factor tab or the Change in Multiple Factors tab to measure how changes greater than 10 % affect the computed values of life-cycle costs.

Figure 4-12 presents a saved sensitivity analysis from the Change in Multiple Factors tab for simultaneous changes in the baseline value of eleven factors. The upper portion of Figure 4-12 largely reproduces the Results section from the Change in Multiple Factors tab (see Figure 4-4). The lower portion of Figure 4-12 records the factor names along with the range for which life-cycle costs are calculated and the corresponding Best Case, Baseline, and Worst Case values of that factor. When all factors are set at their Best Case or Worst Case values, they result in the life-cycle cost values recorded in the upper portion of Figure 4-12.

Figure 4-13 presents a saved Monte Carlo simulation. The upper portion of Figure 4-13 largely reproduces the Results section from the Monte Carlo Simulation window (see

Figure 4-6). The lower portion of Figure 4-13 records the eleven factor names along with the probability distribution and the corresponding Minimum, Baseline, and Maximum values of that factor.

Most Significant Factors		
	Change in Life-Cycle Cost	
Factor	-10%	+10%
BC: Base Case -- Basic Renovation: Discount Rate (7.00%)	+$242,953	-$219,387
Alt. 3: Proposed Alternative – Enhanced Chem/Bio Protection: Discount Rate (7.00%)	+$179,134	-$161,800
Alt. 1: Proposed Alternative – Enhanced Security: Discount Rate (7.00%)	+$171,960	-$155,435
Alt. 2: Proposed Alternative – Enhanced Bio Protection: Discount Rate (7.00%)	+$154,495	-$139,622
BC: Base Case -- Basic Renovation: Site Security: Unit Cost ($125,000)	-$152,931	+$152,931
Alt. 2: Proposed Alternative – Enhanced Bio Protection: Enhanced Renovation: Unit Cost	-$150,000	+$150,000
Alt. 1: Proposed Alternative – Enhanced Security: Enhanced Renovation: Unit Cost	-$150,000	+$150,000
Alt. 3: Proposed Alternative – Enhanced Chem/Bio Protection: Enhanced Renovation: Unit	-$150,000	+$150,000
Alt. 2: Proposed Alternative – Enhanced Bio Protection: Site Security: Unit Cost ($100,000)	-$122,345	+$122,345
Alt. 3: Proposed Alternative – Enhanced Chem/Bio Protection: Site Security: Unit Cost	-$122,345	+$122,345
Alt. 1: Proposed Alternative – Enhanced Security: Site Security: Unit Cost ($100,000)	-$122,345	+$122,345
BC: Base Case -- Basic Renovation: Basic Renovation: Unit Cost ($1,000,000)	-$100,000	+$100,000
Alt. 3: Proposed Alternative – Enhanced Chem/Bio Protection: Electricity: Unit Cost	-$98,107	+$98,107
BC: Base Case -- Basic Renovation: Electricity: Unit Cost ($72,000)	-$83,102	+$83,102
Alt. 2: Proposed Alternative – Enhanced Bio Protection: Electricity: Unit Cost ($70,000)	-$80,794	+$80,794
Alt. 3: Proposed Alternative – Enhanced Chem/Bio Protection: Improved Productivity (IAQ):	-$69,921	+$69,921
Alt. 1: Proposed Alternative – Enhanced Security: Electricity: Unit Cost ($60,000)	-$69,252	+$69,252
BC: Base Case -- Basic Renovation: Telecom Services: Unit Cost ($40,000)	-$46,614	+$46,614
Alt. 2: Proposed Alternative – Enhanced Bio Protection: Improved Productivity (IAQ): Unit	-$46,614	+$46,614
Alt. 3: Proposed Alternative – Enhanced Chem/Bio Protection: GPAC: Unit Cost ($100,000)	-$44,710	+$44,710
Alt. 3: Proposed Alternative – Enhanced Chem/Bio Protection: Telecom Services: Unit Cost	-$41,953	+$41,953
Alt. 2: Proposed Alternative – Enhanced Bio Protection: Telecom Services: Unit Cost	-$41,953	+$41,953
Alt. 1: Proposed Alternative – Enhanced Security: Telecom Services: Unit Cost ($36,000)	-$41,953	+$41,953
Alt. 3: Proposed Alternative – Enhanced Chem/Bio Protection: HVAC/Electrical Mods: Unit	-$30,000	+$30,000
BC: Base Case -- Basic Renovation: Identity Theft: Unit Cost ($100,000)	-$23,150	+$23,150
BC: Base Case -- Basic Renovation: Identity Theft: Unit Cost ($75,000)	-$21,071	+$21,071
Alt. 2: Proposed Alternative – Enhanced Bio Protection: Site Protection: Unit Cost ($200,000)	-$20,000	+$20,000
Alt. 3: Proposed Alternative – Enhanced Chem/Bio Protection: Site Protection: Unit Cost	-$20,000	+$20,000
Alt. 1: Proposed Alternative – Enhanced Security: Site Protection: Unit Cost ($200,000)	-$20,000	+$20,000
Alt. 3: Proposed Alternative – Enhanced Chem/Bio Protection: Improved Productivity (IAQ):	+$15,920	-$16,438
BC: Base Case -- Basic Renovation: Telecom Services: Escalation (0.00%)	-$10,613	+$10,958
Alt. 2: Proposed Alternative – Enhanced Bio Protection: Improved Productivity (IAQ):	+$10,613	-$10,958

Figure 4-11   Most Significant Factors Page of the Uncertainty Report for the Case Study

61

Change in Multiple Factors
Saved Results #1

	Base Case	Alternative 1	Alternative 2	Alternative 3
Best Case	$3,851,247	$3,742,291	$3,473,936	$3,926,667
Baseline	$4,642,554	$4,358,912	$4,254,211	$4,858,660
Worst Case	$5,632,330	$5,119,641	$5,242,637	$6,051,547

INCLUDED FACTORS:

Factor	Range	Best Case	Baseline	Worst Case
Discount Rate	+/-25%	8.75%	7.00%	5.25%
Base Case				
Basic Renovation: Unit Cost	+/-15%	$850,000	$1,000,000	$1,150,000
Site Security: Unit Cost	+/-10%	$112,500	$125,000	$137,500
Alternative 1				
Enhanced Renovation: Unit Cost	+/-10%	$1,350,000	$1,500,000	$1,650,000
Site Security: Unit Cost	+/-10%	$90,000	$100,000	$110,000
Alternative 2				
Enhanced Renovation: Unit Cost	+/-10%	$1,350,000	$1,500,000	$1,650,000
Improved Productivity (IAQ): Unit Cost	+/-50%	-$60,000	-$40,000	-$20,000
Site Security: Unit Cost	+/-10%	$90,000	$100,000	$110,000
Alternative 3				
Enhanced Renovation: Unit Cost	+/-10%	$1,350,000	$1,500,000	$1,650,000
Improved Productivity (IAQ): Unit Cost	+/-50%	-$90,000	-$60,000	-$30,000
Site Security: Unit Cost	+/-10%	$90,000	$100,000	$110,000

Figure 4-12   Summary of Life-Cycle Costs and Factor Values of a Saved Change in Multiple Factors Page of the Uncertainty Report for the Case Study

Monte Carlo Simulation Summary
Saved Set #1

Economic Measure		Statistical Measure						Standard
	Minimum	25%	50%	75%	Maximum	Mean	Deviation
Base Case							
LCC	$3,613,680	$4,239,557	$4,686,909	$5,226,470	$6,170,996	$4,755,419	$605,387
Alternative 1							
LCC	$3,548,538	$4,135,615	$4,446,539	$4,832,411	$5,599,695	$4,491,620	$446,945
Alternative 2							
LCC	$3,385,169	$4,069,376	$4,395,746	$4,720,479	$5,758,714	$4,415,196	$429,627
Alternative 3							
LCC	$3,921,800	$4,634,657	$5,018,948	$5,429,921	$6,429,516	$5,048,609	$506,308

INCLUDED FACTORS				
Factor	Distribution	Lower Bound	Baseline	Upper Bound
Discount Rate	Uniform	4.00%	7.00%	10.00%
Base Case				
Basic Renovation: Unit Cost	Triangular	$800,000	$1,000,000	$1,300,000
Site Security: Unit Cost	Triangular	$110,000	$125,000	$145,000
Alternative 1				
Enhanced Renovation: Unit Cost	Triangular	$1,250,000	$1,500,000	$2,000,000
Site Security: Unit Cost	Triangular	$90,000	$100,000	$115,000
Alternative 2				
Enhanced Renovation: Unit Cost	Triangular	$1,250,000	$1,500,000	$2,000,000

Figure 4-13   **Summary of Life-Cycle Costs, Probability Distributions, and Factor Values of a Saved Monte Carlo Simulation Page of the Uncertainty Report for the Case Study**

5 Analyze Results and Recommend a Cost-Effective Risk Mitigation Plan

Choosing among alternatives designed to reduce the impacts of natural and man-made hazards is more complicated than most building investment decisions. Consequently, guidance is provided to help identify key characteristics and the level of effort that will promote a better-informed decision.

5.1 Employ a Structured Process to Generate a Recommendation

Review the calculated values of each alternative's measures of performance. Include the outcomes computed for each of the three types of analysis: (1) baseline analysis (i.e., fixed parameter values); (2) sensitivity analyses; and (3) Monte Carlo simulations.

Use the performance criterion from each selected evaluation method to rank order alternatives for each type of analysis (baseline analysis, sensitivity analyses, and Monte Carlo simulations). Document differences in alternative rankings among the three types of analysis. Focus on circumstances under which the most cost-effective risk mitigation plan identified in the baseline analysis is replaced by another alternative (other alternatives) when the effects of uncertainty are considered. Use the results of the Monte Carlo simulations to identify the characteristics associated with ranking changes for those alternatives under consideration.

Recommend an alternative as the most cost-effective risk mitigation plan. Provide a rationale for the recommendation. Include as part of the rationale, findings from each of the three types of analysis. Include a discussion of circumstances under which the recommended alternative did not have the best measure of economic performance.

Describe any significant effects that remain unquantified. Explain how these effects impact the recommended alternative. Refer to ASTM Standard Practice E 1765 and its adjunct for guidance on how to present unquantified effects along with the computed values of the measures of economic performance.[18]

5.2 Prepare Report with Documentation Supporting Recommended Risk Mitigation Plan

In a report of an economic evaluation, state the objective, the constraints, the alternatives considered, the key assumptions and data, and the computed value for each outcome (measure of economic performance) of each alternative. Make explicit the discount rate; the study period; the main categories of cost data, including initial costs, recurring and nonrecurring costs, and resale values; and grants and incentives if integral to the decision-making process. State the method of treating inflation. Specify the assumptions or costs that have a high degree of uncertainty and are likely to have a significant impact on the

---

[18] ASTM International. "Standard Practice for Applying the Analytical Hierarchy Process (AHP) to Multiattribute Decision Analysis of Investments Related to Buildings and Building Systems," E 1765, *Annual Book of ASTM Standards: 2006.* Vol. 04.12. West Conshohocken, PA: ASTM International.

results of the evaluation. Document the sensitivity of the results to these assumptions or data. Describe any significant effects that remain unquantified in the report.

5.2.1 Suggested Format for Summarizing Results

Use the generic format for reporting the results of an economic evaluation described in ASTM Standard Guide E 2204.[19] It provides technical persons, analysts, and researchers a tool for communicating results in a condensed format to management and non-technical persons. The generic format calls for a description of the significance of the project, the analysis strategy, a listing of data and assumptions, and a presentation of the computed values of any measures of economic performance. Figure 5-1 uses ASTM Standard Guide E 2204 to produce a concise and comprehensive summary of the alternative risk mitigation strategies for the data center case study.

Figure 5-1 contains three sections. Section 1 sets the stage for summarizing the results that follow; it has two headings. The information called for under these headings discusses the objective of the project. Section 2, Analysis Strategy, has two headings. The information presented under the first heading focuses on documenting the steps taken to ensure that the analysis strategy is logical and complete. The information presented under the second heading focuses on summarizing the key data elements and associated assumptions needed to calculate the values reported in Section 3. Section 3, How Key Measures Are Calculated, Summarized, and Traced, has three headings. The first heading calls for information that provides enough detail on the calculation of key measures for others to understand how the calculated values were produced. The second heading calls for the calculated values for life-cycle costs for each alternative as well as the calculated values for each of the Proposed Alternatives of present value net savings, savings-to-investment ratio, and adjusted internal rate of return. The third heading calls for information to ensure traceability; it includes cited references to specific ASTM standards or any other standards, codes, or regulations used.

The material presented in Sections 1 and 2 of Figure 5-1 provides senior management or other key decision makers with a basic understanding of the problem being analyzed and the steps being taken to address it. For example, Section 1 describes the characteristics of the data center, the hazards it faces, and the renovation strategies designed to address those hazards. Section 2 describes in words the four key measures of economic performance—life-cycle cost, present value net savings, savings-to-investment ratio, and adjusted internal rate of return—and lays out the key data and assumptions that drive the economic evaluation. Section 3.a presents the results of the baseline analysis and the Monte Carlo simulation, both of which indicate that the Enhanced Security alternative and the Enhanced Bio Protection alternative are cost effective. Note that the Enhanced Bio Protection alternative is preferred to the Enhanced Security alternative in most but not all instances.

---

[19] ASTM International. "Standard Guide for Summarizing the Economic Impacts of Building-Related Projects," E 2204, *Annual Book of ASTM Standards: 2006*. Vol. 04.12. West Conshohocken, PA: ASTM International.

Figure 5-1   Summary of the Data Center Case Study

1.a Significance of the Project:

The data center undergoing renovation is a single-story structure located in a suburban community. The floor area of the data center is 3 716 m² (40 000 ft²). The replacement value of the data center is $20 million for the structure plus its contents. The data center contains financial records that are in constant use by the firm and its customers. Thus, any interruption of service will result in both lost revenues to the firm and potential financial hardship for the firm's customers.

The building owners employ four different renovation strategies. The first, referred to as the Basic Renovation, employs upgrades that meet the minimum building performance and security requirements. The second, Enhanced Security, results in enhanced security as well as selected improvements in building performance. The third, Enhanced Bio Protection, provides a high level of protection against particles (biological agents) but no gaseous (chemical agents) protection. The fourth, Enhanced Chem/Bio Protection, provides a high level of protection against particles and gaseous agents. All of the alternatives recognize that in the post-9/11 environment the data center faces heightened risks in two areas. These risks are associated with the vulnerability of information technology resources and the potential for damage to the facility and its contents from chemical, biological, radiological, and explosive (CBRE) hazards. Two scenarios—the potential for a cyber attack and the potential for a CBRE attack—are used to capture these risks.

1.b Key Points:

1. The objective of the renovation project is to provide cost-effective operations and security protection for the data center.
2. The renovation is to upgrade the data center's HVAC, telecommunications and data processing systems and several security-related functions.
3. Four upgrade alternatives are proposed:
   - Basic Renovation
   - Enhanced Security, augments the Basic Renovation by strengthening portions of the exterior envelope, limiting vehicle access to the site, and improving the building's HVAC, data processing and telecommunications systems.
   - Enhanced Bio Protection, augments Enhanced Security by making the building more air tight, installing a high-performance particle filtration system, and modifying electrical feeders.
   - Enhanced Chem/Bio Protection, augments Enhanced Security by making the building more air tight, installing a high-performance particle and gaseous filtration system, and modifying electrical feeders.

2. Analysis Strategy: How Key Measures are Estimated

The following economic measures are calculated as present-value (PV) amounts:
(1) **Life-Cycle Costs** (LCC) for the Base Case (Basic Renovation) and for the Proposed Alternative (Enhanced Renovation), including all costs of acquiring and operating the data center over the length of the study period. The selection criterion is lowest LCC.
(2) **Present Value Net Savings** (PVNS) that will result from selecting the lowest-LCC alternative.   PVNS > 0 indicates an economically worthwhile project.

Additional measures:
(1) **Savings-to-Investment Ratio** (SIR), the ratio of savings from the lowest-LCC to the extra investment required to implement it. A ratio of SIR >1 indicates an economically worthwhile project.
(2) **Adjusted Internal Rate of Return** (AIRR), the annual return on investment over the study period. An AIRR > discount or hurdle rate indicates an economically worthwhile project.

Data and Assumptions:
- The Base Date is 2006.
- The alternative with the lower first cost (Basic Renovation) is designated the Base Case.
- The study period is 25 years and ends in 2030.
- The discount or hurdle rate is 7.0 % real.
- The minimum acceptable rate of return is 7.0 % real.
- Annual probabilities for the outcomes for each attack scenario are given along with outcome costs.
- Annual probabilities and outcome costs differ by renovation strategy.

Figure 5-1 Summary of the Data Center Case Study (Cont.)

3.a Calculation of Savings, Costs, and Additional Measures

Results of Baseline Analysis (Savings and Costs in Thousands of Dollars ($K))

Economic Measure	Base Case	Alt 1	Alt 2	Alt 3
Life-Cycle Cost	$4 643	$4 359	$4 254	$4 859
Investment Cost	$1 150	$1 765	$1 935	$2 153
Delta Investment Cost	N/A	$616	$785	$1 003
Non-Investment Cost	$3 493	$2 593	$2 319	$2 706
Savings	N/A	$899	$1 173	$787
Present Value Net Savings	N/A	$284	$388	-$216
Savings to Investment Ratio	N/A	1.46	1.49	0.78
AIRR	N/A	8.63 %	8.73 %	5.97 %

Results of Monte Carlo Simulation (Savings and Costs in Thousands of Dollars ($K))

Economic Measure	Statistical Measure				
	Minimum	Median	Maximum	Mean	Standard Deviation
LCC_{BC}	$3 614	$4 687	$6 171	$4 755	$605
$LCC_{Alt\ 1}$	$3 549	$4 447	$5 600	$4 492	$447
$LCC_{Alt\ 2}$	$3 385	$4 396	$5 759	$4 415	$430
$LCC_{Alt\ 3}$	$3 922	$5 019	$6 430	$5 049	$506
$PVNS_{Alt\ 1}$	-$5	$239	$587	$264	$160
$PVNS_{Alt\ 2}$	$77	$291	$662	$340	$182
$PVNS_{Alt\ 3}$	-$434	-$332	-$77	-$293	$108

3.b Key Results

*LCC (Thousands of Dollars ($K))

Basic Renovation	$4 643
Enhanced Security	$4 359
Enhanced Bio Protection	$4 254
Enhanced Chem/Bio Protection	$4 859

*PVNS (Thousands of Dollars ($K))

Enhanced Security	$284
Enhanced Bio Protection	$388
Enhanced Chem/Bio Protection	-$216

*SIR

Enhanced Security	1.46
Enhanced Bio Protection	1.49
Enhanced Chem/Bio Protection	0.78

*AIRR

Enhanced Security	8.63 %
Enhanced Bio Protection	8.73 %
Enhanced Chem/Bio Protection	5.97 %

3.c Traceability

Life-cycle costs and supplementary measures were calculated according to ASTM standards E917, E964, E1057, and E 1074.

Treatment of uncertainty and measures of project risk were calculated according to ASTM standards E 1369 and E 1946.

5.2.2 Creating the Executive Summary Report

The generic format is a convenient means for summarizing the purpose, data, assumptions, and results of the economic evaluation. Its function is that of an abstract; it summarizes the important points. The Executive Summary Report supplements the generic format by providing the type of information needed to make a better informed decision.

The Executive Summary Report is created via a dialog box. The dialog box is reached by selecting the *Executive* option under the *Reports* node on the Main Menu. Figure 5-2 shows how the dialog box looks when first opened.

Figure 5-2   Dialog Box for Creating the Executive Summary Report

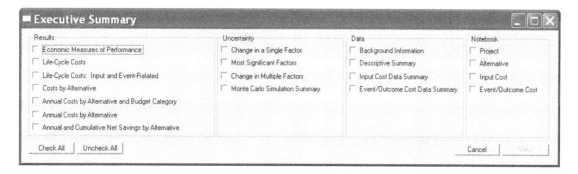

The flow of information in the Executive Summary Report follows the analysis process—baseline analysis, sensitivity analysis, Monte Carlo simulations. Emphasis is first placed on presenting and documenting results; supporting information is then presented.

Referring to Figure 5-2, we see that individual sections of each Report option can be selected or deselected. If all sections are desired, select *Check All*. Groups of sections can be deselected by clicking *Uncheck All*. To examine the Executive Summary Report as it will appear when printed, select *View*.

The "front-end" of the Executive Summary Report includes the user selected sections from the Results Report. Recall that the Results Report presents the results of the baseline analysis. Decision makers may find some sections under the Results heading of greater interest than others. We recommend that the first four sections—Economic Measures of Performance, Life-Cycle Costs, Life-Cycle Costs: Input and Event-Related, and Costs by Alternative—be selected in all cases because they provide a frame of reference for everything that follows.

Next are the results of the sensitivity analysis and the Monte Carlo simulations from the Uncertainty Report. Because the treatment of uncertainty is so important in developing a cost-effective risk mitigation plan, we recommend that the last two sections—Change in Multiple Factors and Monte Carlo Simulation Summary—be selected in all cases.

The third part of the Executive Summary Report presents selected material from the Data Report. Here the emphasis is on documenting the information underpinning the baseline analysis. We recommend that all four sections—Background Information, Descriptive Summary, Input Cost Data Summary, and Event/Outcome Cost Data Summary—be included because they provide the kind of information that will help decision makers have confidence in the data and assumptions that shaped the economic evaluation.

To complete the Executive Summary Report, include as supporting documentation information compiled from the risk assessment and a description of the process by which combinations of risk mitigation strategies were assembled. This information is contained in the Project Notebook. Once again, we recommend that all four sections—Project, Alternatives, Input Costs, and Event/Outcome Costs—be included because they provide the kind of information that will help decision makers have confidence in the data and assumptions that shaped the economic evaluation. Also contained in the Project Notebook is information tied to the critical resource documents (e.g., the reports produced by the risk assessment team or a condition assessment prepared by an architectural/engineering firm containing recommended mitigation strategies and cost estimates for implementing them), which enables analysts to quickly locate key documents and plans if they are requested by the decision maker.

6   Next Steps

Now that you have completed the guided tour, use the test files that you created to gain familiarity with the software. Experiment with the various means for editing, creating, and deleting data elements. Create simple applications using your own data to master the full capabilities of the Cost-Effectiveness Tool. Build more complex applications and use the sensitivity analysis and Monte Carlo simulation features to evaluate how changing the values of key inputs affect economic performance. Use the Results Report to learn how to drill down on key cost drivers and use that information to help guide you in conducting and saving additional sensitivity analyses and Monte Carlo simulations. Have as a goal to use the software as a decision support tool; it is largely self documenting, it lays out the information going into the analysis, and provides guidance in choosing a cost-effective risk mitigation plan.

Visit the OAE website to learn about future updates and pending software releases.

Appendix A   Technical Considerations

An economic evaluation may be divided into four stages: (1) identification; (2) classification; (3) quantification; and (4) presentation. The identification stage identifies the investment alternatives to be evaluated. The identification stage involves identifying and listing all of the "effects" of the alternatives being analyzed. In principle, this set of effects produces a checklist of all items that should be taken into consideration. The second stage entails classifying these effects into investment and non-investment cost categories. The third stage produces year-by-year estimates of the values of each of the cost categories. The final stage is the presentation and analysis of the measures of economic performance in a form that clearly details the important assumptions underlying the economic evaluation and the implications of these assumptions for the study's conclusions.

Once all costs have been identified and classified, it becomes necessary to develop year-by-year estimates for each of the cost categories for each alternative under analysis. We denote the alternatives as A_j (where the index for j ranges from $0, ..., N$, for a total of $N+1$ alternatives).

Each alternative under consideration meets certain feasibility requirements. First, it must satisfy all of the specified functional requirements. Second, it must not exceed any stated budget constraints. The first requirement insures that all technical criteria (e.g., thermal performance and indoor air quality) and all regulatory constraints (e.g., building codes and standards) are met. The second requirement excludes any proposals which cannot be implemented due to insufficient funds.

The material presented in this appendix assumes that all alternatives are feasible in that they meet the functional requirements and have been screened vis-à-vis any stated budget constraints. Thus, there is no requirement that alternatives be optimally configured, although the evaluation methods presented in this chapter are all applicable to choosing among a set of optimally configured alternatives.

Associated with each alternative are investment cost categories k (where the index k ranges from $1, ..., K_j$) and non-investment cost categories m (where the index m ranges from $1, ..., M_j$). The potential for future terrorist attacks, as well as other natural and man-made hazards, are measured by the expected value of annual losses. Associated with each alternative are expected loss categories p (where the index p ranges from $1, ..., P_j$). Some of the expected loss categories accrue to investment costs and some accrue to non-investment costs. Expected losses are modeled separately from investment costs and non-investment costs to better characterize the nature of low-probability, high-consequence events.[20]

It is important to note that some costs entering the analysis may be negative. For example, the salvage and sale of equipment and components at the end of the study

---

[20] The information needed to perform the expected loss calculations is a byproduct of the risk assessment and the identification of potential mitigation strategies.

period result in a salvage value whose present value equivalent is subtracted from other investment costs. Similarly, improvements to indoor air quality may result in productivity improvements which favorably impact occupants; these "savings" are subtracted from non-investment costs. Any pure benefits which result (e.g., increased rental income due to improvements) are subtracted from non-investment costs (i.e., benefits are treated as negative costs).

At the heart of the economic evaluation methodology is an economic concept referred to as the time value of money. This concept relates to the changing purchasing power of money as a result of inflation or deflation, along with consideration of the real earning potential of alternative investments over time. The discount rate reflects the decision maker's time value of money. The discount rate is used to convert, via a process known as discounting, costs which occur at different times to a base time. Throughout this report, the term "present value" will be used to denote the value of a cost found by discounting cash flows (present and future) to the base time. The base time is the date (base year) to which costs are converted to time equivalent values.

In order to describe each of the four standardized methods of economic performance—life-cycle cost, present value of net savings, savings-to-investment ratio, and adjusted internal rate of return—we define a series of terms.

t $=$ a unit of time;[21]

T $=$ the length of the study period in years;

d $=$ the discount rate expressed as a decimal.

The prefix, PV, is used to designate dollar denominated quantities in present value terms. The present value is derived by discounting (i.e., using the discount rate) to adjust all costs—present and future—to the base year (i.e., $t = 0$). The present value terms are: the present value of investment costs (PVI), the present value of non-investment costs (PVC), and the present value of expected losses ($PVE(L)$). Because $PVE(L)$ includes some loss categories which accrue to investment costs and some which accrue to non-investment costs, we denote the present value of investment costs inclusive of losses as PVI' and the present value of non-investment costs inclusive of losses as PVC'.

The cost terms that make up the mathematical formulations for the four standardized methods are given in Equations (A.1) through (A.6). While there may be many different ways of classifying costs (i.e., classification schemes), their explicit treatment in both the mathematical formulation and the standardized methods ensures that a close coupling results between the mathematical formulation and each standardized method.

The investment costs for alternative A_j in year t are expressed as:

---

[21] Denote the beginning of the study period as the base year (i.e., $t = 0$) and end of the study period as T. Thus, the length of the study period in years is T.

$$I_{jt} = \sum_{k=1}^{K_j} I_{kjt} \qquad\qquad\qquad (A.1)$$

where I_{kjt} = the estimated cost accruing to the kth investment cost category for alternative A_j in year t.

The non-investment costs for alternative A_j in year t are expressed as:

$$C_{jt} = \sum_{m=1}^{M_j} C_{mjt} \qquad\qquad\qquad (A.2)$$

where C_{mjt} = the estimated cost accruing to the mth non-investment cost category for alternative A_j in year t.

The expected losses for alternative A_j in year t may now be expressed as:

$$E\left(L_{jt}\right) = \sum_{p=1}^{P_j} E\left(L_{pjt}\right) \qquad\qquad\qquad (A.3)$$

where L_{pjt} = the expected loss accruing to the pth loss category for alternative A_j in year t.

The present value of investment costs for alternative A_j are expressed as:

$$PVI_j = \sum_{t=0}^{T} \left(\sum_{k=1}^{K_j} I_{kjt} \right) / (1+d)^t \qquad\qquad\qquad (A.4)$$

The present value of non-investment costs for alternative A_j are expressed as:

$$PVC_j = \sum_{t=0}^{T} \left(\sum_{m=1}^{M_j} C_{mjt} \right) / (1+d)^t \qquad\qquad\qquad (A.5)$$

The present value of expected losses for alternative A_j are expressed as:

$$PVE\left(L_j\right) = \sum_{t=0}^{T} \left(\sum_{p=1}^{P_j} E\left(L_{pjt}\right) \right) / (1+d)^t \qquad\qquad\qquad (A.6)$$

A.1   Life-Cycle Cost Method Formulas

The life-cycle cost (LCC) method measures, in present-value or annual-value terms, the sum of all relevant costs associated with owning and operating a constructed facility over a specified period of time. The basic premise of the LCC method is that to an investor or decision maker all costs arising from that investment decision are potentially important to that decision, including future as well as present costs. Applied to constructed facilities, the LCC method encompasses all relevant costs over a designated study period, including the costs of designing, purchasing/leasing, constructing/installing, operating, maintaining, repairing, replacing, and disposing of a particular design or system. Should any pure benefits result (e.g., increased rental income due to improvements), include them in the calculation of LCC.

The LCC method is particularly suitable for determining whether the higher initial cost of a constructed facility or system specification is economically justified by lower future costs (e.g., losses due to natural or manmade hazards) when compared to an alternative with a lower initial cost but higher future costs. If a design or system specification has both a lower initial cost and lower future costs relative to an alternative, an LCC analysis is not needed to show that the former is economically preferable.

The LCC for alternative A_j may now be expressed as:

$$LCC_j = \sum_{t=0}^{T} \left(\sum_{k=1}^{K_j} I_{kjt} + \sum_{m=1}^{M_j} C_{mjt} + \sum_{p=1}^{P_j} E\left(L_{pjt}\right) \right) / (1+d)^t \tag{A.7}$$

The LCC for alternative A_j may also be expressed in present value terms as:

$$LCC_j = PVI_j + PVC_j + PVE\,(L_j) \tag{A.8}$$

or, by explicitly including losses in investment costs and non-investment costs, as:

$$LCC_j = PVI'_j + PVC'_j \tag{A.9}$$

Denote the alternative with the lowest initial investment cost (i.e., first cost) as A_0; it is referred to as the base case. Then:

$$I_{00} < I_{j0} \quad \text{for } j = 1, ..., N \tag{A.10}$$

The LCC method compares alternative, mutually exclusive, designs or system specifications that satisfy a given functional requirement on the basis of their life-cycle costs to determine which is the least-cost means (i.e., minimizes life-cycle cost) of satisfying that requirement over a specified study period. With respect to the base case, alternative A_j is economically preferred if, and only if, $LCC_j < LCC_0$.

A.2   Present Value of Net Savings Formula

The present value of net savings (PVNS) method is reliable, straightforward, and widely applicable for finding the economically efficient choice among investment alternatives.

It measures the net savings from investing in a given alternative instead of investing in the foregone opportunity (e.g., some other alternative or the base case).

The PVNS for a given alternative, A_j, vis-à-vis the base case, A_0, may be expressed as:

$$PVNS_{j:0} = LCC_0 - LCC_j \tag{A.11}$$

Any pure benefits that result (e.g., increased rental income due to improvements) are included in the calculation of PVNS, since they are included in the LCC calculation.

With respect to the base case, if $PVNS_{j:0}$ is positive, alternative A_j is economic; if it is zero, the investment is as good as the base case; if it is negative, the investment is uneconomical.

A.3 Savings-to-Investment Ratio Formulas

The savings-to-investment ratio (SIR) is a numerical ratio whose size indicates the economic performance of a given alternative instead of investing in the foregone opportunity. The SIR is savings divided by investment costs. The LCC method provides all of the necessary information to calculate the SIR. The SIR for a given alternative, A_j, is calculated vis-à-vis the base case. The numerator and denominator of the SIR are derived through reference to Equation (A.9).

The numerator equals the difference in the present value of non-investment costs inclusive of losses between the base case and the given alternative, A_j. The resultant expression, denoted as present value of savings, is given by.

$$PVS_{j:0} = PVC'_0 - PVC'_j \tag{A.12}$$

The denominator equals the difference in the present value of investment costs inclusive of losses for the given alternative, A_j, and the base case.[22] The resultant expression, denoted as present value of increased investment costs, is given by:

$$PVII_{j:0} = PVI'_j - PVI'_0 \tag{A.13}$$

The SIR for a given alternative, A_j, vis-à-vis the base case may be expressed as:

$$SIR_{j:0} = \frac{PVS_{j:0}}{PVII_{j:0}} \tag{A.14}$$

---

[22] Do not use the savings-to-investment ratio as a decision criterion if $PVI'_j \leq PVI'_0$. See Appendix C of Chapman and Leng for a discussion of this and other topics associated with the calculation of the savings-to-investment ratio. Chapman, Robert E., and Leng, Chi J. *Cost-Effective Responses to Terrorist Risks in Constructed Facilities*. NISTIR 7073 (Gaithersburg, MD: National Institute of Standards and Technology, 2004).

A ratio less than 1.0 indicates that A_j is an uneconomic investment relative to the base case; a ratio of 1.0 indicates an investment whose benefits or savings just equal its costs; and a ratio greater than 1.0 indicates an economic project. Readers interested in a mathematical derivation of the SIR calculation and how to interpret the calculated value of the SIR for three special cases are referred to Appendix C of Chapman and Leng.

A.4   Adjusted Internal Rate of Return Formula

The adjusted internal rate of return (AIRR) is the average annual yield from a project over the study period, taking into account reinvestment of interim receipts. Because the AIRR calculation explicitly includes the reinvestment of all net cash flows, it is instructive to introduce a new term, terminal value (TV). The terminal value of an investment, A_j, is the future value (i.e., the value at the end of the study period) of reinvested net cash flows excluding all investment costs. The terminal value for an investment, A_j, is denoted as TV_j.

The reinvestment rate in the AIRR calculation is equal to the minimum acceptable rate of return (MARR), which is assumed to equal the discount rate, d, a constant. When the reinvestment rate is made explicit, all investment costs are easily expressible as a time equivalent initial outlay (i.e., a value at the beginning of the study period) and all non-investment cash flows as a time equivalent terminal amount. This allows a straightforward comparison of the amount of money that comes out of the investment (i.e., the terminal value) with the amount of money put into the investment (i.e., the time equivalent initial outlay).

The AIRR is defined as the interest rate, r_j, applied to the terminal value, TV_j, which equates (i.e., discounts) it to the time equivalent value of the initial outlay of investment costs. It is important to note that all investment costs are discounted to a time equivalent initial outlay using the discount rate, d.

Several procedures exist for calculating the AIRR. These procedures are derived and described in detail in the report by Chapman and Fuller.[23] The most convenient procedure for calculating the AIRR is based on its relationship to the SIR. This procedure results in a closed-form solution for a given alternative, A_j, vis-à-vis the base case, $r_{j:0}$. The AIRR is that value of $r_{j:0}$ for which:

$$r_{j:0} = (1+d)(SIR_{j:0})^{\frac{1}{T}} - 1 \qquad (A.15)$$

With regard to the base case, if $r_{j:0}$ is greater than the discount rate (also referred to as the hurdle rate), alternative A_j is economic; if $r_{j:0}$ equals the discount rate, the investment is as good as the base case; if $r_{j:0}$ is less than the discount rate, the investment is uneconomical.

---

[23] Chapman, Robert E. and Fuller, Sieglinde K. *Benefits and Costs of Research: Two Case Studies in Building Technology*. NISTIR 5840 (Gaithersburg, MD: National Institute of Standards and Technology, 1996).

Appendix B Glossary of Terms

Adjusted Internal Rate of Return (AIRR): The average annual yield from a project over the study period, taking into account reinvestment of interim receipts. The reinvestment rate in the AIRR calculation is equal to the discount rate.

> Notes:
> (1) See Section 2.3.4 and Appendix A.4.
> (2) Output window – cost summary
> (3) Input windows – cost summary (pull-down menu)
>
> Example:
> In the provided case study, the proposed alternative, Enhanced Security, has an AIRR of 8.6 %.

AIRR: See Adjusted Internal Rate of Return.

Alternatives: Means by which costs and events/outcomes sequences for various risk mitigation plans are differentiated. Once owners and managers assess the risk of natural and manmade hazards to the constructed facility, they must identify potential strategies to mitigate this risk. The identification includes potential risk mitigation measures and predictions of the effectiveness and costs of these measures. The final step in the protocol for creating a risk mitigation plan is economic evaluation of the risk mitigation alternatives.

> Notes:
> (1) See Section 2.2.
> (2) Output window – cost summary
> (3) Input windows – alternatives, capital investment cost information, O&M cost information, other cost information, event information
> (4) Reports – data (alternative information – descriptive summary), uncertainty (change in a single factor, most significant factors), results (alternative information – descriptive summary)
>
> Example:
> The case study compares the base case (basic renovation) *alternative* with the proposed (enhanced renovation) *alternative*.

Amount: Attribute of cost, which is calculated as the quantity of a cost item (capital investment, O&M, or other cost) multiplied by its unit cost.

Notes:
(1)   Reports – data (alternative information – input cost data summary, event/outcome cost data summary)

Example:
An O&M filter replacement cost item of quantity 75 with a unit cost of $100 will yield an *amount* of $7 500.

Annual Value: A uniform annual amount equivalent to the project costs or benefits taking into account the time value of money throughout the study period. Life-cycle costs may be expressed in either annual value terms or present value terms.

Annually Recurring: Means of classifying/allocating costs that occur every year within the frequency of occurrence choices of the CET software for O&M or other cost items. The three occurrence frequency choices are *annually recurring*, periodic (other than annual), and aperiodic.

Notes:
(1)   See Section 3.2.1.1; see also Figure 3-9.
(2)   Input windows – O&M cost information, other cost information

Example:
In the provided case study, site security is an O&M cost that is *annually recurring* throughout the study period.

Aperiodic: Means of classifying/allocating costs that follow an irregular schedule (not strictly periodic) within the frequency of occurrence choices of the CET software for O&M or other cost items. The three occurrence frequency choices are annually recurring, periodic (other than annual), and *aperiodic*.

Notes:
(1)   See Section 3.2.1.1; see also Figure 3-9.
(2)   Input windows – O&M cost information, other cost information

Example:
In the provided case study, duct cleaning is an *aperiodic* O&M cost item incurred in year 17.

Baseline Analysis: The starting point for conducting an economic evaluation. In the baseline analysis, all data elements entering into the calculations are fixed. The term baseline analysis is used to denote a complete analysis in all respects but one; it does not address the effects of uncertainty.

Notes:
(1)   See Section 2.4.1 and Chapter 3.
(2)   Output window – cost summary
(3)   Reports – data, uncertainty, results

Example:
In the *Data Center Case Study.lcc* file, the data elements displayed on the various
software screens are the baseline values.

Base Year (Time): The date to which all future and past benefits/costs are converted
when a present or annual value method is used.

Notes:
(1)   See Appendix A.
(2)   Input windows – project description
(3)   Reports – data (background information), results (background
        information)

Example:
2006 is the assigned *base year* in the case study. All cash flows are discounted to
a 2006 dollar value.

Bearer of Costs: One of the four dimensions by which costs are classified in the detailed
cost-accounting framework (*bearer of costs*; budget category; building/facility
component; mitigation strategy). Means by which cost items are assigned to the group
that is responsible for shouldering the cost burden. There are three bearer categories:
owner/manager, occupant/user, third party.

Notes:
(1)   See Section 2.5; see also Figure 2-1.
(2)   Output window – cost summary
(3)   Input windows – capital investment cost information, O&M cost
        information, other cost information, event/outcome cost information
(4)   Reports – data (alternative information – input cost data summary,
        event/outcome cost data summary), results (summary of life-cycle costs,
        summary of costs by alternative)

Example:
The case study cost item, basic renovation is a capital investment assigned to the
owner/manager as the cost bearer.

Budget Category: One of the four dimensions by which costs are classified in the detailed cost-accounting framework (bearer of costs; *budget category*; building/facility component; mitigation strategy). *Budget category* is defined as one of three cost types: capital investment, O&M (operations and maintenance), other.

Notes:
(1)   See Section 2.5; see also Figure 2-1.
(2)   Output window – cost summary
(3)   Input windows – edit costs/events
(4)   Reports – data (alternative information – input cost data summary, event/outcome cost data summary), results (summary of life-cycle costs, summary of costs by alternative)

Example:
In the provided case study, enhanced renovation is a cost item assigned to the capital investment *budget category*.

Building Decision: A decision regarding the design, financing, engineering, construction, management, or operation of a building.

Building/Facility Component: One of the four dimensions by which costs are classified in the detailed cost-accounting framework (bearer of costs; budget category; *building/facility component*; mitigation strategy). *Building/facility component* is defined as one of three cost types: building/facility elements; building/facility site work; non-elemental. The first two cost types are associated with the elemental classification UNIFORMAT II.

Notes:
(1)   See Section 2.5; see also Figure 2-1.
(2)   Output window – cost summary
(3)   Input windows – capital investment cost information, O&M cost information, other cost information, event/outcome cost information
(4)   Reports – data (alternative information – input cost data summary, event/outcome cost data summary), results (summary of life-cycle costs, summary of costs by alternative)

Example:
In the provided case study, site security is a non-elemental *building/facility component* cost item.

Building/Facility Elements: One of the three cost types that define the building/facility component of the detailed cost-accounting framework: *building/facility elements*;

building/facility site work; non-elemental. The *building/facility elements* cost type is associated with the elemental classification UNIFORMAT II.

Notes:
(1)   See Section 2.5; see also Figure 2-1.
(2)   Output window – cost summary
(3)   Input windows – capital investment cost information, O&M cost information, other cost information, event/outcome cost information
(4)   Reports – data (alternative information – input cost data summary, event/outcome cost data summary), results (summary of life-cycle costs, summary of costs by alternative)

Example:
In the provided case study, HVAC upgrade is a cost item assigned to the *building/facility elements* cost type.

Building/Facility Site Work: One of the three cost types that define the building/facility component of the detailed cost-accounting framework: building/facility elements; *building/facility site work*; non-elemental. The *building/facility site work* cost type is associated with the elemental classification UNIFORMAT II.

Notes:
(1)   See Section 2.5; see also Figure 2-1.
(2)   Output window – cost summary
(3)   Input windows – capital investment cost information, O&M cost information, other cost information, event/outcome cost information
(4)   Reports – data (alternative information – input cost data summary, event/outcome cost data summary), results (summary of life-cycle costs, summary of costs by alternative)

Example:
In the provided case study, site lighting is a cost item assigned to the *building/facility site work* cost type.

Capital Investment: One of the three cost types that define the budget category classification: *capital investment*, O&M (operations and maintenance), other. The cost of acquiring, substantially improving, expanding, changing the functional use of, or replacing a building or building system. *Capital investment* costs accrue to the investment cost category, while O&M and other costs accrue to the non-investment cost category.

Notes:
(1)   See Section 2.5; see also Figure 2-1.
(2)   Output window – cost summary

(3)   Input windows – edit costs/events

(4)   Reports – data (alternative information – input cost data summary, event/outcome cost data summary), results (summary of life-cycle costs, summary of costs by alternative, summary of annual costs by alternative and budget category)

Example:
In the provided case study, basic renovation is a cost item assigned to the *capital investment* budget category.

Cash Flow: The stream of monetary (dollar) values – benefits and costs – resulting from a project investment.

Notes:
(1)   See Appendix A.

(2)   Reports – data (alternative information – input cost data summary, event/outcome cost data summary), results (summary of annual costs by alternative and budget category, summary of annual costs by alternative)

Classification Information: The group of associated attributes for a given cost, including: bearer, budget category, component, and mitigation strategy.

Notes:
(1)   See Section 3.2.1.1 and Section 3.2.1.2.

(2)   Input windows – capital investment cost information, O&M cost information, other cost information, event/outcome cost information

(3)   Reports – data (alternative information – input cost data summary, event/outcome cost data summary), results (summary of life-cycle costs, summary of costs by alternative)

Example:
In the provided case study, basic renovation is a cost item with the following *classification information*: bearer – owner/manager, budget category – capital investment, mitigation strategy – engineering alternatives, component – building/facility elements.

Constant Dollar Analysis: Dollars of uniform purchasing power exclusive of general inflation or deflation; based on the value of a dollar in a specified base year.

Notes:
(1)   See Section 3.2.1.

(2)   Output window – cost summary

(3)   Input windows – project description

(4)   Reports – data (background information), results (background information)

Example:
In the provided case study, the costs are estimated and analyzed based on the value of a dollar in the assigned base year of 2006.

Constructed Facilities: Permanent structures, including infrastructure, buildings, and industrial facilities.

Copy Alternative: Command that allows an existing alternative to be copied another alternative (e.g., Base Case to Alternative 1; Alternative 1 to Alternative 2; etc.). Once copied to another alternative, the "duplicate" copy is accessible for editing.

Notes:
(1)   Input windows – alternative description

Copy Cost: Command that allows an existing cost to be copied. The copy is accessible for editing and use only within the alternative to which the original cost item was assigned.

Notes:
(1)   Input windows – edit costs/events

Example:
Repairs to air handling units may share many of the same attributes as the HVAC repairs that have been defined within the case study. Thus, *copy cost* allows the user to make a copy of HVAC repairs that can later be revised/edited to reflect specifics of repairing air handling units.

Copy Event: Command that allows an existing event to be copied. The copy is accessible for editing and use only within the alternative to which the original event was assigned.

Notes:
(1)   Input windows – edit costs/events

Example:
In the case study, cyber attack (years 11-25) shares all attributes with cyber attack (years 1-10) except for the assigned years. Thus, the *copy event* command could be used to make a copy of cyber attack (years 1-10) and edited slightly to yield the event cyber attack (years 11-25).

Cost-Accounting Framework: Methodology for tracking how costs affect stakeholders in different ways. The cost-accounting framework promotes a detailed, consistent breakdown of life-cycle costs.

> Notes:
> (1)   See Section 2.5; see also Figure 2-1.
> (2)   Output window – cost summary
> (3)   Reports – data (alternative information – input cost data summary, event/outcome cost data summary), results (summary of life-cycle costs, summary of costs by alternative)

Cost Effective: The condition whereby the present value benefits (savings) of an investment exceeds its present value costs.

> Notes:
> (1)   See Section 2.3.1; see also Sections 2.3.2, 2.3.3, and 2.3.4.
> (2)   Reports – results (summary of life-cycle costs, summary of annual costs by alternative)

> Example:
> In the provided case study, the proposed alternative is the cost-effective investment choice because it has the lowest life-cycle cost.

Cost Item: Name/description assigned to a cost associated with a given alternative and a specific bearer, budget category, component, and mitigation strategy. Information on cost items is needed in order to calculate life-cycle costs. *Cost items* are classified under two broad headings: input costs and event-related costs.

> Notes:
> (1)   See Section 2.5; see also Figure 3-8 and Figure 3-14.
> (2)   Input windows – capital investment cost information, O&M cost information, other cost information, event/outcome cost information
> (3)   Reports – data (alternative information – input cost data summary, event/outcome cost data summary), uncertainty (change in a single factor, most significant factors), results (summary of costs by alternative)

> Example:
> In the case study, basic renovation is a *cost item* associated with the base case alternative that embodies the following attributes: bearer – owner/manager, budget category – capital investment, component – building/facility elements, mitigation strategy – engineering alternatives.

Cost Summary Window: Main screen in the CET program that provides a snapshot of the costs associated with each alternative in regards to cost classification information.

> Notes:
> (1)   Output window – cost summary
> (2)   Input windows – capital investment cost information, O&M cost information, other cost information, event/outcome cost information

Current Dollar Analysis: Analysis of the costs incurred in dollars of purchasing power in which actual prices are stated (not corrected for inflation or deflation).

> Notes:
> (1)   See Section 3.2.1.
> (2)   Output window – cost summary
> (3)   Input windows – project description
> (4)   Reports – data (background information), results (background information)

Data Report: Report that organizes all user inputted data for each project alternative. Useful method of checking that all values were inputted correctly previous to conducting further analyses.

> Notes:
> (1)   *Data Report* includes: background information; alternative information – descriptive summary, input cost data summary, event/outcome cost data summary

Delete All Costs: Command that allows all existing costs associated with a specific alternative to be deleted.

> Notes:
> (1)   Input windows – edit costs/events

Delete All Events: Command that allows all existing events associated with a specific alternative to be deleted.

> Notes:
> (1)   Input windows – edit costs/events

Delete Cost: Command that allows an existing cost to be deleted from the associated alternative.

    Notes:
    (1)   Input windows – edit costs/events

Delete Event: Command that allows an existing event to be deleted from the associated alternative.

    Notes:
    (1)   Input windows – edit costs/events

Descriptive Summary: Section appearing in both the data report which provides a summary of each project alternative and the associated outcomes.

    Notes:
    (1)   Report – data (alternative information – descriptive summary)

Disaster Mitigation: Measures, procedures, and strategies designed to reduce either the likelihood or consequences of a disaster.

    Notes:
    (1)   See Section 3.2.1.1.
    (2)   Output window – cost summary
    (3)   Input windows – project description, alternatives
    (4)   Reports – data (background information), results (background information)

Discount Rate: The rate of interest reflecting the investor's time value of money, used to determine discount factors for converting benefits and costs occurring at different times to a base year. The discount rate may be expressed as nominal or real.

    Notes:
    (1)   See Appendix A.
    (2)   Input windows – project description
    (3)   Reports – data (background information), results (background information)

    Example:
    In the provided case study, a real *discount rate* is used; it is assigned a value of 7.0 %. This value is used to adjust costs incurred in different years to the value of a dollar in the base year, 2006.

Edit Costs/Events: Command that allows the user to edit attributes of an existing cost or event (including create new, copy, or delete).

> Notes:
> (1) Output window – cost summary
> (2) Input windows – edit costs/events

Edit Outcomes: Command that allows the user to edit attributes of an existing outcome (including create new, copy, or delete).

> Notes:
> (1) Input windows – event information, edit outcomes/outcome costs

Engineering Alternatives: One of the three mitigation strategy classifications (*engineering alternatives*; management practices; financial mechanisms). Technical options in the construction or renovation of constructed facilities, their systems, or their subsystems to reduce the likelihood or consequences of disasters; types of engineering alternatives include designs, materials, components.

> Notes:
> (1) See Section 2.5; see also Figure 2-1.
> (2) Output window – cost summary
> (3) Input windows – capital investment cost information, O&M cost information, other cost information, event/outcome cost information
> (4) Reports – data (alternative information – input cost data summary, event/outcome cost data summary), results (summary of life-cycle costs, summary of costs by alternative)

> Example:
> In the case study, the HVAC upgrade is a capital investment that employs an *engineering alternatives* mitigation strategy.

Escalation Rate: The rate of change in price for a particular good or service (as contrasted with the inflation rate, which is for all goods and services).

> Notes:
> (1) See Section 3.2.1.1 and Section 3.2.1.2.
> (2) Input windows – capital investment cost information, O&M cost information, other cost information, event/outcome cost information
> (3) Reports – data (alternative information – input cost data summary, event/outcome cost data summary)

(4)   If the value of the *escalation rate* entered was 0.0 % and a *sensitivity analysis* is requested for that factor, then a notice appears indicating that the percentage range will be tied to the inflation rate.

Example:
In the provided case study, the *escalation rate* associated with the O&M cost item site lighting is –0.10 %. This indicates that the value of the cost incurred will be adjusted by this percentage before being factored into the life-cycle cost of the project.

Event Description: Section that allows the user to enter more specific information about the circumstances/details of a specified event.

Notes:
(1)   Input windows – event information
(2)   Reports – data (alternative information – descriptive summary), results (alternative information – descriptive summary)

Example:
The *event description* for the event Cyber attack specifies the parameters that qualify as a cyber attack.

Event Information: Window that allows the user to input/alter data defining an event associated with a specific alternative (includes description and occurrence years).

Notes:
(1)   Input windows – event information

Example:
The *event information screen* allows the user to input pertinent information that differentiates cyber attack (years 11-25) from cyber attack (years 1-10).

Executive Summary Report: Report that organizes all user-generated data, intermediate calculations, and results for presentation to senior management or other decision makers. The report is constructed through a dialog box, where the user selects the appropriate sections for inclusion. Use the Executive Summary Report to support the recommendation of one alternative as the most cost-effective risk mitigation plan.

Notes:
(1)   *Executive Summary Report* includes: background information; alternative information – descriptive summary, input cost data summary, event/ outcome cost data summary; economic measures of performance; summary of life-cycle costs; summary of life-cycle costs: input and event-

related; summary of costs by alternative; summary of annual costs by alternative and budget category; summary of annual costs by alternative; summary of annual and cumulative net savings by alternative; saved sensitivity analyses; most significant factors; saved Monte Carlo simulations; and Project Notebook.

Externality: The discrepancy between private and social costs or private and social benefits.

Financial Mechanisms: One of the three mitigation strategy classifications (engineering alternatives; management practices; *financial mechanisms*). A set of devices relating to finances that facility owners and managers can utilize to reduce their exposure to natural and man-made hazards. These devices include purchase of insurance policies and responding to external financial incentives to engage in engineering-based or management-based risk mitigation.

    Notes:
    (1)   See Section 2.5; see also Figure 2-1.
    (2)   Output window – cost summary window
    (3)   Input windows – capital investment cost information, O&M cost information, other cost information, event/outcome cost information
    (4)   Reports – data (alternative information – input cost data summary, event/outcome cost data summary), results (summary of life-cycle costs, summary of costs by alternative)

    Example:
    Financial mechanisms that serve as incentives include government subsidies for investments to harden a facility and rental premiums paid by tenants who value the facility's added safety features.

First (Initial) Costs: Attribute of a capital investment. Costs incurred in placing a building or building subsystem into service, including, but not limited to, costs of planning, design, engineering, site acquisition and preparation, construction, purchase, installation, property taxes and interest during the construction period, and construction-related fees.

    Notes:
    (1)   See Section 2.3.1; see also Section 3.2.1.1 and Figure 3-8.
    (2)   Input windows – capital investment cost information
    (3)   Reports – data (input costs data summary)

    Example:

In the provided case study, basic renovation is a *first cost* cost item because it is incurred in order to place the building into use.

Inflation: A rise in the general price level over time, usually expressed as a percentage rate.

> Notes:
> (1)   See Section 3.2.1.

Investment Cost: First cost and later expenditures which have substantial and enduring value (generally more than one year) for upgrading, expanding, or changing the functional use of a building or building system.

> Notes:
> (1)   See Section 2.5.

> Example:
> In the provided case study, HVAC upgrade is classified as an *investment cost* because, as a modernization of an existing system, it is a long-term investment.

Key Parameters: Grouping of attributes related to a specific event outcome (probability of outcome, first year, and last year).

> Notes:
> (1)   Input windows – event information, outcome information
> (2)   Reports – data (alternative information – descriptive summary), results (alternative information – descriptive summary).

> Example:
> In the provided case study, the minor damage outcome linked to the CBRE attack for the basic renovation alternative is defined by the following *key parameters*: probability of occurrence, 0.5 %; first year, 2006; last year, 2030

LCC: See Life-Cycle Cost.

Life-Cycle Cost (LCC): A technique of economic evaluation that sums over a given study period the costs of initial investment (less resale value), replacements, operation (including energy use) and maintenance of an investment decision. Life-cycle costs may be expressed in either present value terms or annual value terms.

> Notes:

(1)   See Section 2.3.1 and Appendix A.1.
(2)   Output window – cost summary
(3)   Input windows – cost summary (pull-down menu)
(4)   Reports – results (summary of life-cycle costs, summary of costs by alternatives, summary of annual costs by alternative and budget category, summary of annual costs by alternative)

Example:
The base case alternative in the case study has a *life-cycle cost* of $4 642 554, taking into account the present value costs/benefits of all cash flows throughout the study period.

Management Practices: One of the three mitigation strategy classifications (engineering alternatives; *management practices*; financial mechanisms). Practices employed by building owners and managers to reduce the risks associated with natural and man-made hazards. These practices can be procedural or technical and related to security, training, communications, site location, and systems access, among others. Some *management practices* complement engineering alternatives, while others substitute for them.

Notes:
(1)   See Section 2.5; see also Figure 2-1.
(2)   Output window – cost summary
(3)   Input windows – capital investment cost information, O&M cost information, other cost information, event/outcome cost information
(4)   Reports – data (alternative information – input cost data summary, event/outcome cost data summary), results (summary of life-cycle costs, summary of costs by alternative)

Example:
In the case study, site security is an O&M cost that employs a *management practice* mitigation strategy.

Mitigation Strategy: One of the four core components of the cost-accounting framework (bearer of costs; budget category; building/facility component; *mitigation strategy*). Means of classifying/allocating costs within the CET software in regards to risk management. The three *mitigation strategy* classifications include engineering alternatives; management practices; financial mechanisms.

Notes:
(1)   See Section 2.5; see also Figure 2-1.
(2)   Output window – cost summary
(3)   Input windows – capital investment cost information, O&M cost information, other cost information, event/outcome cost information

93

(4)   Reports – data (alternative information – input cost data summary, event/outcome cost data summary), results (summary of life-cycle costs, summary of costs by alternative)

Example:
In the provided case study, the HVAC upgrade is a capital investment that employs an engineering alternatives *mitigation strategy.*

Monte Carlo Simulation: A means for addressing the effects of uncertainty. Monte Carlo simulation varies a small set of data inputs according to an experimental design. Associated with each data input is a probability distribution function from which values are randomly sampled. A Monte Carlo simulation complements the *baseline analysis* by evaluating the changes in output measures when selected data inputs are allowed to vary about their baseline values.

Notes:
(1)   See Section 2.4.3 and Section 4.2.
(2)   Input window – Monte Carlo (Include Factors).
(3)   Output window – Monte Carlo (Results).
(4)   Reports – uncertainty (saved Monte Carlo simulations).

Nominal Discount Rate: The rate of interest reflecting the time value of money stemming both from inflation and the real earning power of money over time. This is the discount rate used in discount formulas or in selecting discount factors when future benefits and costs are expressed in current dollars.

Notes:
(1)   Input windows – project description
(2)   Reports – data (background information), results (background information)

Non-Elemental: One of the three cost types that define the building/facility component of the detailed cost-accounting framework: building/facility elements; building/facility site work; *non-elemental. Non-elemental* costs are all costs that cannot be attributed to specific functional elements of the project.

Notes:
(1)   See Section 2.5; see also Figure 2-1.
(2)   Output window – cost summary
(3)   Input windows – capital investment cost information, O&M cost information, other cost information, event/outcome cost information

(4)   Reports – data (alternative information – input cost data summary, event/outcome cost data summary), results (summary of life-cycle costs, summary of costs by alternative)

Example:
An example of a non-elemental/capital/owner cost item is the purchase of a right-of-way, or easement.

O&M (Operations and Maintenance): One of the three cost types that define the budget category classification: capital investment, *O&M (operations and maintenance)*, other. Cost items falling under the *O&M* cost type include energy and water costs, maintenance and repair costs, minor replacements related to maintenance and repair, and insurance premiums paid by owners and/or occupants to reduce their risk exposure. *O&M* costs are usually paid from an annual operating budget, not from capital funds, and accrue to the non-investment cost category.

Notes:
(1)   See Section 2.5; see also Figure 2-1.
(2)   Output window – cost summary
(3)   Input windows – edit costs/events
(4)   Reports – data (alternative information – input cost data summary, event/outcome cost data summary), results (summary of life-cycle costs, summary of costs by alternative, summary of annual costs by alternative and budget category)

Example:
In the provided case study, HVAC repairs is a cost item attributed to the *O&M* budget category.

Occupant/User: One of three bearer categories: owner/manager, *occupant/user*, third party. Specifically, the burden of the associated cost falls on the facility user or occupant. *Occupant/User* costs frequently include operations and maintenance costs and selected types of repairs not covered by the project's owner or agent. *Occupant/User* costs can also include delay costs and business interruption costs due to temporary closures for repair and reconstruction activities.

Notes:
(1)   See Section 2.5; see also Figure 2-1.
(2)   Output window – cost summary
(3)   Input windows – capital investment cost information, O&M cost information, other cost information, event/outcome cost information
(4)   Reports – data (alternative information – input cost data summary, event/outcome cost data summary), results (summary of life-cycle costs, summary of costs by alternative)

Example:
The case study the cost item, HVAC repairs is an O&M cost assigned to the *occupant/user* as the cost bearer.

Operating Cost: The expenses incurred during the normal operation of a building or a building system or component, including labor, materials, utilities, and other related costs.

Other Costs: One of the three cost types that define the budget category classification: capital investment, O&M (operations and maintenance), *other*. *Other* costs are non-capital costs that cannot be attributed to the O&M cost type.

Notes:
(1)   See Section 2.5; see also Figure 2-1.
(2)   Output window – cost summary
(3)   Input windows – edit costs/events
(4)   Reports – data (alternative information – input cost data summary, event/outcome cost data summary), results (summary of life-cycle costs, summary of costs by alternative, summary of annual costs by alternative and budget category)

Example:
In the provided case study, change in traffic pattern is a cost item attributed to the *other* budget category.

Outcome Description: Section that allows the user to enter more specific information about the circumstances/details/probability of a specified event *outcome*.

Notes:
(1)   Input windows – outcome information
(2)   Reports – data (alternative information – descriptive summary), results (alternative information – descriptive summary)

Example:
The *outcome description* for the minor damages Cyber attack *outcome* specifies the parameters that qualify a cyber attack as minor as opposed to major damages.

Owner/Manager: One of three bearer categories: *owner/manager*, occupant/user, third party. Specifically, the burden of the associated cost falls on the facility owner or manager. *Owner/Manager* costs are all costs incurred by the project's owner or agent.

These costs include but are not limited to design costs, capital investment costs, and selected types of repairs to the constructed facility.

Notes:
(1) See Section 2.5; see also Figure 2-1.
(2) Output window – cost summary
(3) Input windows – capital investment cost information, O&M cost information, other cost information, event/outcome cost information
(4) Reports – data (alternative information – input cost data summary, event/outcome cost data summary), results (summary of life-cycle costs, summary of costs by alternative)

Example:
The case study cost item, site protection, is a capital investment cost assigned to the *owner/manager* as the cost bearer.

Periodic (other than annual): Means of classifying/allocating O&M and other costs that occur on a scheduled timeframe other than on an annual basis. The three occurrence frequency choices are annually recurring, *periodic (other than annual)*, and aperiodic.

Notes:
(1) See Section 3.2.1.1; see also Figure 3-10.
(2) Input windows – O&M cost information, other cost information

Example:
The case study cost item, HVAC repairs, is an O&M cost incurred every 6 years in the proposed alternative, Enhanced Security.

Present Value: The value of a benefit or cost found by discounting future cash flows to the base year. Life-cycle costs may be expressed in either present value terms or annual value terms.

Notes:
(1) See Appendix A.
(2) Output window – cost summary

Example:
The base case alternative in the case study has a life-cycle cost of $4 642 554, taking into account the *present value* costs/benefits of all cash flows throughout the study period.

Present Value Net Savings (PVNS): A method for finding the economically efficient choice among investment alternatives. It measures the net savings from investing in a

97

given alternative instead of investing in the foregone opportunity (e.g., some other alternative or the base case). The PVNS for a given alternative, A_j, vis-à-vis the base case, A_0, may be expressed as: $PVNS_{j:0} = LCC_0 - LCC_j$.

Notes:
(1) See Section 2.3.2 and Appendix A.2.
(2) Output window – cost summary
(3) Input windows – cost summary (pull-down menu)

Example:
In the provided case study, the proposed alternative, Enhanced Security, results in a PVNS of $283 642.

Probability of Occurrence: Provides the chance that a there will be a specific outcome associated with a given event. The sum of all outcome probabilities for a single event must be equal to 1. Listed as one of the three key parameters for a given outcome: *probability of occurrence*, first year, last year.

Notes:
(1) See Section 3.2.1.2.
(2) Input windows – outcome information
(3) Reports – data (alternative information – descriptive summary), results (alternative information – descriptive summary)

Example:
In the provided case study, the major damage outcome for the CBRE attack event is assigned a probability of 0.05 %.

Project: Resources and activities used to achieve a specific set of objectives within a specified time schedule.

Notes:
(1) See Section 2.2; see also Section 2.6.
(2) Input windows – project description
(3) Output window – cost summary
(4) Reports – data, uncertainty, results

Project Notebook: Report containing data and information associated with the risk assessment and the formulation of risk mitigation strategies stemming from the risk assessment. The Project Notebook is an important resource for documenting the sources of key data elements.

PVNS: See Present Value Net Savings.

Quantity: Attribute of cost items that specifies the number of units that require installation or replacement. The amount displayed for a cost is the multiplicative product of *quantity* and unit cost.

Notes:
(1)   See Section 3.2.1.1 and Section 3.2.1.2.
(2)   Input windows – capital investment cost information, O&M cost information, other cost information, event/outcome cost information

Example:
In the case study, the salvage and sale of equipment and components is assigned a *quantity* of 1.

Real Discount Rate: The rate of interest reflecting that portion of the time value of money related to the real earning power of money over time. This is the discount rate used in discount formulas or in selecting discount factors when future benefits and costs are expressed in constant dollars.

Notes:
(1)   See Section 3.2.1; see also Section 2.6.3.
(2)   Input windows – project description
(3)   Reports – data (background information), results (background information)

Example:
In the provided case study, the *real discount rate* is assigned a value of 7.0 %, which is used to calculate life-cycle costs. This value is used to adjust costs incurred in different years to the value of a dollar in the base year, 2006.

Replacement Costs: Building component replacement and related costs, included in the capital budget, that are expected to be incurred during the study period.

Notes:
(1)   See Section 2.5.

Example:
In the provided case study, the HVAC upgrade for the proposed alternative, Enhanced Security, is a $30 000 *replacement cost* incurred in year 17.

Resale Value: The monetary sum expected from the disposal of an asset at the end of its economic life, its useful life, or at the end of the study period.

> Notes:
> (1)   See Section 2.5.

Results Report: Report that summarizes the results of the economic evaluation. The report provides a series of measures of project performance. The report provides a summary of life-cycle costs using the cost-accounting framework as well as detailed present value tabulations on all cost items. The report provides annual cash flows (expressed in base year present value dollars) for each budget category and overall for each alternative.

> Notes:
> (1)   *Results Report* includes: economic measures of performance; summary of life-cycle costs; summary of life-cycle costs: input and event-related; summary of costs by alternative; summary of annual costs by alternative and budget category; summary of annual costs by alternative; summary of annual and cumulative net savings by alternative

Retrofit: The modification of an existing building or facility to include new systems or components.

> Notes:
> (1)   See Section 2.6.1 and Section 2.6.2.
>
> Example:
> In the provided case study, both the basic renovation and the enhanced renovation are considered a *retrofit* of the existing facility.

Risk Analysis: The body of theory and practice that has evolved to help decision makers assess their risk exposures and risk attitudes so that the investment that is "best for them" is selected.

Risk Mitigation: The actions or decisions designed to reduce the financial and nonpecuniary risk from uncertain events.

> Notes:
> (1)   See Section 2.5; see also Figure 2-1.

Salvage Value: The value of an asset, assigned for tax computation purposes, that is expected to remain at the end of the depreciation period (represented as a negative cost value). One of three time classification attributes of a capital investment: initial, future, salvage.

> Notes:
> (1)   See Section 2.5; see also Section 3.2.1 and Figure 3-8.
> (2)   Input windows – capital investment cost information
>
> Example:
> In the provided case study, the *salvage value* for the HVAC upgrade in the proposed alternative, Enhanced Security, is -$12 500.00; it occurs in year 25, the final year of the study period.

Savings-to-Investment Ratio (SIR): Either the ratio of present value savings to present value investment costs, or the ratio of annual value savings to annual value investment costs.

> Notes:
> (1)   See Section 2.3.3 and Appendix A.3.
> (2)   Output window – cost summary
> (3)   Input window – cost summary (pull-down menu)
>
> Example:
> In the provided case study, the proposed alternative, Enhanced Security, has an SIR of 1.46.

Sensitivity Analysis: A means for addressing the effects of uncertainty. A test of the outcome of an analysis by altering one or more parameters (key data elements or input variables) from (an) initially assumed value(s). A *sensitivity analysis* complements the *baseline analysis* by evaluating the changes in output measures when selected data inputs are allowed to vary about their baseline values.

> Notes:
> (1)   See Section 2.4.2 and Section 4.1.
> (2)   Input window – sensitivity analysis, change in single factor tab (range), most significant factors tab (compute), change in multiple factors tab (range)
> (3)   Output window – sensitivity analysis, change in single factor tab (results), most significant factors tab, change in multiple factors tab (results)
> (4)   Reports – uncertainty (saved sensitivity analyses, most significant factors)

SIR: See Savings-to-Investment Ratio.

Study Period: The length of time over which an investment is analyzed.

> Notes:
> (1)   See Appendix A.
> (2)   Input windows – project description
> (3)   Reports – data (background information), results (background information)

> Example:
> The provided case analyzes the life-cycle costs of alternative data center renovation strategies over a 25 year *study period*, from 2006 to 2030.

Third Party: One of three bearer categories: owner/manager, occupant/user, *third party*. Specifically, the burden of the associated cost falls on a party other than the facility owner or user. Natural hazards, industrial accidents, and terrorist acts that occur infrequently, but whose consequences are devastating, highlight the importance of including the *Third Party* cost type in the private sector's life-cycle cost calculus.

> Notes:
> (1)   See Section 2.5; see also Figure 2-1.
> (2)   Output windows – cost summary
> (3)   Input windows – capital investment cost information, O&M cost information, other cost information, event/outcome cost information
> (4)   Reports – data (alternative information – input cost data summary, event/outcome cost data summary), results (summary of life-cycle costs, summary of costs by alternative)

> Example:
> An example of a *third party* cost is the lost sales for a business establishment whose customer access has been impeded (e.g., due to a road closure during construction/reconstruction).

Triangular Distribution: A probability distribution often used in a *Monte Carlo simulation*. Specification of the triangular distribution requires three data points, the minimum value, the most likely value, and the maximum value. In CET 4.0, the most likely value is set equal to the baseline value. The triangular distribution is recommended whenever the range of input value is finite and continuous and a clustering about some central value is expected.

> Notes:
> (1)   See Section 4.2.
> (2)   Input window – Monte Carlo (Include Factors).

(3)   Output window – Monte Carlo (Results).

(4)   Reports – uncertainty (saved Monte Carlo simulations).

Uncertainty Report: Report containing saved results from the Change in a Single Factor tab, the Most Significant Factors tab, Change in Multiple Factors tab, and Monte Carlo Simulation tab. Useful in supporting a recommendation of an alternative as the most cost-effective risk mitigation plan.

Notes:

(1)   *Uncertainty Report* includes: saved sensitivity analyses; most significant factors; and saved Monte Carlo simulations.

Uniform Distribution: A probability distribution often used in a *Monte Carlo simulation*. Specification of the uniform distribution requires two data points, the minimum value and the maximum value. All values between the minimum and maximum are equally likely. The uniform distribution is recommended whenever the range of input values is finite and continuous but no clustering about a central value is expected.

Notes:

(1)   See Section 4.2.

(2)   Input window – Monte Carlo (Include Factors).

(3)   Output window – Monte Carlo (Results).

(4)   Reports – uncertainty (saved Monte Carlo simulations).

UNIFORMAT II: An elemental format based on major components common to most buildings. It serves as a consistent reference for analysis, evaluation, and monitoring of buildings during the planning, feasibility, and design stages. It also enhances reporting at all stages in construction. The two cost types, building/facility elements and building/facility site work, under the building/facility component cost classification are associated with the elemental classification *UNIFORMAT II*. Subcategories under *UNIFORMAT II* include: substructure, shell, interiors, services, equipment & furnishings, special construction/demolition.

Notes:

(1)   See Section 2.5.

(2)   See ASTM International. "Standard Classification for Building Elements and Related Site Work—UNIFORMAT II," E 1557, *Annual Book of ASTM Standards: 2006.* Vol. 04.11. West Conshohocken, PA: ASTM International.

(3)   Input windows – capital investment cost information, O&M cost information, other cost information, event/outcome cost information

Unit Cost: Attribute of cost items that specifies a cost per unit that require installation or replacement. The amount displayed for a cost is the multiplicative product of quantity and *unit cost*.

> Notes:
> (1)   See Section 3.2.1.1 and Section 3.2.1.2.
> (2)   Input windows – capital investment cost information, O&M cost information, other cost information, event/outcome cost information
>
> Example:
> In the case study, the cost of HVAC repairs under the Basic Renovation alternative is assigned a *unit cost* of $5 000.

Year Cost Incurred (Timing): Attribute of cost items that specifies when a cost is incurred.

> Notes:
> (1)   See Section 3.2.1.1 and Section 3.2.1.2.
> (2)   Input windows – capital investment cost information, O&M cost information, other cost information, event information
>
> Example:
> In the case study, the HVAC upgrade is a capital investment specified under the Enhanced Security alternative that is assigned a cost incurred year of 17, which corresponds to the year 2022.

References

ASTM International. "Standard Classification for Building Elements and Related Site Work—UNIFORMAT II," E 1557, *Annual Book of ASTM Standards: 2006.* Vol. 04.11. West Conshohocken, PA: ASTM International.

ASTM International. "Standard Guide for Selecting Economic Methods for Evaluating Investments in Buildings and Building Systems," E 1185, *Annual Book of ASTM Standards: 2006.* Vol. 04.11. West Conshohocken, PA: ASTM International.

ASTM International. "Standard Guide for Selecting Techniques for Treating Uncertainty and Risk in the Economic Evaluation of Buildings and Building Systems," E 1369, *Annual Book of ASTM Standards: 2006.* Vol. 04.11. West Conshohocken, PA: ASTM International.

ASTM International. "Standard Guide for Developing a Cost-Effective Risk Mitigation Plan for New and Existing Constructed Facilities," E 2506, *Annual Book of ASTM Standards: 2006.* Vol. 04.12. West Conshohocken, PA: ASTM International.

ASTM International. "Standard Guide for Summarizing the Economic Impacts of Building-Related Projects," E 2204, *Annual Book of ASTM Standards: 2006.* Vol. 04.12. West Conshohocken, PA: ASTM International.

ASTM International. "Standard Practice for Applying the Analytical Hierarchy Process (AHP) to Multiattribute Decision Analysis of Investments Related to Buildings and Building Systems," E 1765, *Annual Book of ASTM Standards: 2006.* Vol. 04.12. West Conshohocken, PA: ASTM International.

ASTM International. "Standard Guide for Developing a Cost-Effective Risk Mitigation Plan for New and Existing Constructed Facilities," E 2506, *Annual Book of ASTM Standards: 2006.* Vol. 04.12. West Conshohocken, PA: ASTM International.

ASTM International. "Standard Practice for Measuring Benefit-to-Cost and Savings-to-Investment Ratios for Investments in Buildings and Building Systems," E 964, *Annual Book of ASTM Standards: 2006.* Vol. 04.11. West Conshohocken, PA: ASTM International.

ASTM International. "Standard Practice for Measuring Cost Risk of Buildings and Building Systems." E 1946. *Annual Book of ASTM Standards: 2006.* Vol. 04.12. West Conshohocken, PA: ASTM International.

ASTM International. "Standard Practice for Measuring Internal Rate of Return and Adjusted Internal Rate of Return for Investments in Buildings and Building Systems," E 1057, *Annual Book of ASTM Standards: 2006.* Vol. 04.11. West Conshohocken, PA: ASTM International.

ASTM International. "Standard Practice for Measuring Life-Cycle Costs of Buildings and Building Systems," E 917, *Annual Book of ASTM Standards: 2006.* Vol. 04.11. West Conshohocken, PA: ASTM International.

ASTM International. "Standard Practice for Measuring Net Benefits and Net Savings for Investments in Buildings and Building Systems," E 1074, *Annual Book of ASTM Standards: 2006.* Vol. 04.11. West Conshohocken, PA: ASTM International.

Chapman, Robert E. and Fuller, Sieglinde K. *Benefits and Costs of Research: Two Case Studies in Building Technology.* NISTIR 5840 (Gaithersburg, MD: National Institute of Standards and Technology, 1996).

Chapman, Robert E., and Leng, Chi J. *Cost-Effective Responses to Terrorist Risks in Constructed Facilities.* NISTIR 7073 (Gaithersburg, MD: National Institute of Standards and Technology, 2004).

Thomas, Douglas S., and Chapman, Robert E. *A Guide to Printed and Electronic Resources for Developing a Cost-Effective Risk Mitigation Plan for New and Existing Constructed Facilities.* NIST Special Publication 1082 (Gaithersburg, MD: National Institute of Standards and Technology, 2008).